How Not t
Compl
as a N

NOT BY THE AUTHORS

Chicken Soup for the Mouth

What to Expect When You're Expecting to Get a What to Expect Book When You're Expecting

The Crucial First Six Seconds: An Exhaustive Guide to the All-Important First Tenth of a Minute of Your Child's Life

The Even More Crucial Second Six Seconds: Making or Breaking Your Child's Future

The Baby Hollerer

Disciplining Your Child: When to Be Cruel to Be Kind and When to Be Cruel Just Because It's Fun

The *Larry the Worm* Series:
- *Larry the Worm Goes to School*
- *Larry the Worm Continues Going to School*
- *Larry the Worm Does Post-Graduate Work*
- *Larry the Worm Struggles to Pay Off His Student Loan*
- *Embittered Larry the Worm Drives a Cab*

The Book of Dubious Home Remedies for Serious Life-Threatening Injuries for Which You Should Really Call a Doctor

How to Build a Summer Home from Soiled Diapers!

139 Extremely Complicated Steps to Slightly Better Parenting

How Not to Completely Suck as a New Parent

Scott Feschuk and Paul Mather

M&S

National Library of Canada Cataloguing in Publication

Feschuk, Scott
How not to completely suck as a new parent / Scott Feschuk, Paul Mather

ISBN 0-7710-4754-1

1. Parenting – Humor. 2. Canadian wit and humor (English).
I. Mather, Paul, 1968-   II. Title.

PN6231.P2F48 2004   C818'.602   C2003-907295-9

We acknowledge the financial support of the Government of Canada through the Book Publishing Industry Development Program and that of the Government of Ontario through the Ontario Media Development Corporation's Ontario Book Initiative. We further acknowledge the support of the Canada Council for the Arts and the Ontario Arts Council for our publishing program.

Typeset in Minion by M&S, Toronto
Printed and bound in Canada

This book is printed on acid-free paper that is
100% ancient forest friendly (100% post-consumer recycled)

McClelland & Stewart Ltd.
The Canadian Publishers
481 University Avenue
Toronto, Ontario
M5G 2E9
www.mcclelland.com

1 2 3 4 5   08 07 06 05 04

For Muriel Feschuk, a loving and beloved
mother and grandmother
– S. F.

To my wife, Lisa, and my kids, Katie and Sam
– P. M.

CONTENTS

INTRODUCTION

Okay, so you're a parent now. Or you're about to become a parent. Congratulations! This means you have Several Important Things to Remember, the first of which is: You're a parent now. This may seem obvious, what with the baby and all, but trust us, as a new parent, you are going to be forgetting a lot of things. For instance, you'll forget what it felt like to sleep through the night. You'll soon forget that. Your memory just goes. Also, you'll forget what it felt like to sleep through the night. Your memory just goes.

The second Important Thing to Remember is that while being a new parent can imbue the human spirit with a profound and eternal love, it also has more tangible repercussions – namely the remarkable ability to prevent you from doing anything enjoyable at all for the next five years. Forget about eating at nice restaurants. Forget backpacking through Europe. Forget reading books that aren't made of cloth and don't squeak. You're a parent now, and twenty-six hours a day will be filled up with parenting. For the remaining minus two hours, you will be too tired to do anything except watch TV. Sometimes, you'll watch it for several minutes before realizing that it is not on. And at that precise moment, you will finally come to understand why *your* parents were so damn boring.

THE FIRST YEAR

You may be surprised and upset by your newborn's appearance. Don't panic! Many newborn babies have dry flaky skin, bulging eyes, and a slightly pointed head. This is normal and a result of either (a) the birth process, or (b) the fact that you and your partner are both ugly bug-eyed pointy-headed people.

Pointed Head

It's common for a newborn's head to look "squished." This is because travelling headfirst through the birth canal is a traumatic event (slightly less so if you're a baby). Space is at a premium here: the body is twisted and compressed into various unnatural positions. It's like flying economy class, but Mother Nature is merciful and there are no bad Kevin Bacon movies.

As a result of all this twisting and bending and pushing, your baby's head is compressed. This is less of a big deal than it would be for you because your baby has a soft spot at the top of her skull called the fontanelle which allows it to squish up into a point. During the first few months of life this soft spot will grow over and your child will no longer have any holes in her head until she turns fourteen and gets her nose pierced.

Eye and Hair Colour

If you and your partner are Caucasian, you may find your child has a different eye and hair colour than your own. This is totally normal. During the first few years of life Caucasian babies may change eye or hair colour several times, having a new look every few months, much like Madonna.

If your baby's eyes are blue, they may turn brown or green. If they are brown, they may turn blue or grey. If they are red and glowing, you probably just took a family picture with a flash camera. Or your kid might have evil powers. If you and your partner are not Caucasian, but your baby is, you may want to have a word with the hospital.

Birthmarks

Minor birthmarks are usually nothing to be concerned about. Your child may have freckles or small moles. If one of the moles is shaped like a little "666" and your child has the red, glowing eye thing mentioned above, this gives credence to the whole evil-power theory.

Check your child's buttocks for marks as soon as possible. If you find one saying "Mattel," somebody's trying to pull a fast one.

Falling in Love After the Birth

Many fathers may feel uncomfortable holding a small infant. But as the nurse hands over the baby for the first time, it's not uncommon for men to fall in love: the eyes, the hair, the perfect body.

However this is also a good time to look at the baby.

Conclusion

Your newborn may look rough, but as you examine your child you'll see a little bit of yourself. And that's when it will strike home: this little scabby, bald-headed, bug-eyed monster is truly a miracle.

Because if you look anything like *that*, it's miraculous somebody had sex with you in the first place.

Now that you've got a baby, you need a place to put her. A box or a comfy "nest" of dirty clothes by the laundry bin might do nicely at first, but eventually you'll want to construct a nursery for the newest member of your family (hint: that's your baby).

Setting up a nursery doesn't have to be difficult – at least it doesn't if you don't already have the baby. If you've waited until *after* you have had the baby to set up the nursery, man oh man, you're in for a world of hurt. Oh, you can still do it in your spare time, but don't expect to have it finished before the kid turns thirty.

Step One: Where to Put the Nursery?

Where should you set up your nursery? It might be tempting to say "at a neighbour's" but, chances are, various laws and regulations will require you to keep the baby at your own residence.

This can be a puzzler, because most of us don't have extra rooms in the house that aren't currently being used for something. Every room is for an activity, reflecting some function of your life.

Luckily, now that you've had a baby there won't be any more activities, other than taking care of the baby, so many of these rooms are now expendable. Let's see which can go:

The Den: What is a den for? Doing taxes. Smoking a pipe. Staring at that fish mounted on the wall. Or, if you're a bear, sleeping. Dens are pretty expendable, and if your house has one, odds are it's a good choice to become a nursery. Just be sure to let the pipe smoke clear, and for safety's sake be sure to remove that memorable catch from the wall, especially if it's a swordfish.

The Kitchen: The kitchen is a bad choice. Kitchens are used to prepare food, and you will need to prepare food, as you will never eat in a restaurant ever again for the rest of your life.

Actually, that's not true: eventually you will get a night out, but that will be so far in the future that waiters will be robots and food will be served in the form of pills. Try the soylent green, it's excellent.

Front room: Again, maybe not a good choice. Although the front room is used only for sitting around in and relaxing, which – again – you won't be doing any more, there are reasons why it doesn't make a good nursery.

1. Big windows let in too much light and keep baby awake.

2. It's likely adjacent to front door, which is knocked on by Jehovah's Witnesses early in the morning, waking baby up.

3. Actually, if the light is keeping the baby awake then the baby would already be up when the Jehovah's Witnesses knocked so, what the heck, go for it.

Bathroom: An interesting possibility. The bathroom contains many of the necessities of life: water to drink, a place to wash, a toilet, magazines, possibly a homemade toilet-paper cozy that looks like Barbie but with a crocheted skirt that covers the spare roll of toilet paper.

And so a bathroom/nursery would have everything you need to care for your infant: water to mix formula and to wash baby, toilet paper to clean up spills, magazines that can be torn up and used as rudimentary diapers, and that Barbie toilet-paper thing. You could probably throw that out.

However, to make room for the crib and other baby essentials you'd probably have to remove most of the bathroom fixtures. Thus, although you'd have solved the "where to put the nursery?" problem, you would have created the "where to put the bathroom?" problem. As you can see, this could set up an infinite recursion where all the rooms in your house keep shifting around like some gigantic game of Tetris.

A house whose rooms are constantly being renovated and rearranged could be expensive, but on the other hand would make a great TV show for the Home and Garden Network. Do the costs outweigh the benefits? It's up to you to judge.

Spare bedroom: You have a spare bedroom? Great! Let's make that the nursery. Why the hell have you been letting us go through all these other stupid rooms?

Step Two: Walls
Does your new nursery have walls? It should. If not, go back to Step One. Or go to the Home Depot and buy some walls.

You'll want to redecorate your nursery walls by putting up wallpaper, repainting, or doing a paint effect. Why? Because you're stupid. Babies have absolutely no interest in this stuff, and yet you do it. And why is that? Because the powerful wall decoration industry has spent millions on advertising to *poison your mind*.

Come on . . . break free! You don't need to decorate the nursery. Stained white walls are fine! Skip this section and move on. Send a message to those big-shot paint and wallpaper industry tycoons who sit in their mansions trying to tell *you* what to do with your God-given walls. Fight the power!

Can't do it, can you? All right, let's decorate the nursery.

Do you know the sex of the baby? If it's already been born, you should. Here's a breakdown of decorating choices by gender:

Boy: Blue colour scheme. Sports, cowboy, or astronaut motif. Or an astronaut riding on a horse wearing a hockey helmet and holding a baseball, if you want to try to make sure your son doesn't grow up to be gay.

Girl: Pink or pastel colour scheme. Bunny, puppy, or fairy motif. Horses are acceptable as long as they have large dewy eyes and aren't standing near cowboys or knights. Large useless swaths of fabric must decorate all windows.

In the 1970s, a painting of Raggedy Ann was a must for a girl's room, but this is now optional. If desired, Raggedy Ann may be depicted riding a horse or feeding a puppy. She may not be engaged in traditional "boy" activities such as playing baseball, travelling in a rocket ship, or peeing standing up.

Unknown sex: Green or yellow colour scheme. Asexual decoration motif: teddy bears, happy faces, letters of the alphabet, or pictures of David Bowie from the early "Is he a chick or what?" phase of his career.

Twin boys: Really blue walls with mural of two cowboys fighting spacemen with hockey sticks.

Twin girls: Ultra-double-pink walls with posters of bunnies having tea party with knitting fairies. Large swaths of fabric decorating windows, doors, light fixtures, and electrical outlets.

Twins, one boy and one girl: This is a poser. Better not to paint anything and always keep the room dark.

Step Three: Furniture

Your baby will need a place to sleep, a change table, and a place to store clothing. Actually, your baby will just need a place to sleep. *You'll* need a change table and a place to store clothing. Babies are slobs – they'd be okay with getting changed on the dining-room table and having their clothes kept in a big garbage bag in the corner.

Where should your baby sleep? A crib is traditional. A waterbed is not recommended. A hammock is also a bad idea. A water hammock sounds intriguing but, sadly, has not yet been invented.

When choosing a crib be sure to get one that is safe. This is especially important if you are buying an older crib second-hand.

Many older cribs are not compatible with current safety standards. For example, they might use lead-based paint, or be designed in such a way that it's possible for a baby to climb out. In the 1960s, it was common for cribs to have big poisonous spikes, or a button that, when pushed, shot out flames. We now know spikes and flames to be detrimental to babies' health.

You'll also want a change table. Note that change tables are for changing babies, not for storing loose change. Although, if you wish, you may discreetly place a tip jar in one corner. Babies are cheap, though. Yours probably won't tip, no matter how efficiently you perform your services.

Step Four: Finishing Touches

You may wish to decorate your baby's room with a mobile. Babies love mobiles, and can ignore them for hours, especially if they are expensive and battery-operated.

Later, when your baby is a toddler, he will express an interest in the mobile, ripping it out of the ceiling and dragging it around the house, using it to strangle the cat, etc. Watching the dancing colours and shifting patterns of the mobile as the cat struggles for breath can be quite soothing.

You may also wish to get an easy chair, so you can nurse baby in comfort. It's customary to get a rocking chair, or a modified rocking chair known as a glider. But you might want to be non-traditional and get one of those chairs from the sixties that looks like a big white ball that you sit inside. Then you spin around dramatically and say, "Welcome, Mr. Bond, we've been expecting you." Except instead of holding a white cat you're nursing a baby.

Let's see what Bond makes of *that*. Your move, 007!

There isn't much to the first month of life. Sure, birth is a miracle and when you stare into a newborn's eyes you can see infinity, and your newborn child's brain has more connections than there are stars in the universe and she is full of possibilities and so on, but when you get down to it, for the first month at least, they don't *do* much.

Life with your newborn will consist of a cycle involving three activities, with a few sudden, random events. Here is the basic three-activity cycle:

Basic One-Month-Old Activity Cycle
1. Baby eats.
2. Baby burps.
3. Baby sleeps.

At this point you might be asking, "Whoa, did I misread that? Can my newborn really play with a rattle?" Yes, you misread it. Your newborn can't play with a rattle. Or finger puppets. Or that plastic thing with a suction cup you bought at a toy store and you're now waving in front of his squinty little eyes.

Refer again to the list. Does it say "Look at plastic thing with a suction cup recently bought from a toy store"? No, it does not. So put that thing away and get ready for all the eating and burping and sleeping.

Now it's not as monotonous as you might think. Things don't always have to go "eat burp sleep, eat burp sleep." Sometimes baby will eat, *then* sleep, then (after waking up) burp. Sometimes he will burp, then eat, then burp again before more eating and finally going to sleep. Sometimes, amazingly, he will sleep first, then burp, then eat.

If that all sounds more or less like the same thing to you, you're right. It is. Your baby, your wonderful child, is going to do those same three things over and over again for a month, and you are going to watch. So put away the suction-cup thing already.

How can you tell when your baby is transitioning between phases – when he is coming out of, say, the burp zone, and moving into sleeping time? Simple, the baby will indicate that he is passing through this zone of transition by crying. So a more accurate version of our activity cycle would read like this:

Modified One-Month-Old Activity Cycle
1. Baby eats.
1a. Baby cries.
2. Baby burps.
2a. Baby cries.
3. Baby sleeps.
3a. Baby cries.

Maybe this sounds boring, not the exciting world of hijinks and slapstick you were expecting after having seen the *Look Who's Talking* series of movies. Nevertheless, that's what you're in for, not wisecracking fun as voiced by Bruce Willis. If you hear Bruce Willis' voice coming from your infant, check again. Maybe that's actually Bruce Willis. His hair is like that now.

However, from time to time your baby will break out of the routine with one of several exciting bonus behaviours that are programmed to happen at random times, just to keep you as a parent interested. Here are the fun, random bonus activities:

Fun, Random Bonus Activities

1. Baby fills a diaper.
2. Baby pukes on you.

Again, the timing of these events is random. Like a little slot machine, you never know when your baby is going to pay-off. One minute you'll be holding him, about to transition from eating into sleeping and . . . jackpot!

You may look at the above list and say to yourself: "Wow! That's amazing! Is it really true that my one-month-old can smile and say 'I love you'?" No. It is not true. That's not what it says at all. You are really bad at reading lists.

Those of you with better reading skills may have noticed that item one and item two are both similar activities coming from opposite ends. This raises the question: Is it possible for a baby to fill a diaper *while throwing up on you*? In other words, is it possible to get the fabled double jackpot?

Current scientific theories say no. If a baby were to throw up on you while crapping, the forces would balance perfectly and the baby would pop into the fourth dimension or possibly go back in time.

And what would time-travelling baby do if he were thrust back through the centuries to, say, the Old West or the Fall of the Roman Empire? Would he try to change history, or would he just silently observe?

Neither! He's a little baby, remember? Here's what he would do:

What Your Baby Would Do if Thrust Back through Time into the Old West or the Fall of the Roman Empire

1. Eat.
2. Burp.
3. Sleep.

And it wouldn't matter if the Emperor Nero wiggled a suction-cup toy in front of his face, he wouldn't look at it because he's not old enough to focus his eyes. So for the last time, put that thing away!

For the new parent, the world of diapering can be a confusing place. Cloth or disposable? Premium or generic? And is there really such a place as "the World of Diapering"? What kind of stupid name for a planet is that? The questions go on and on.

Should You Diaper Your Baby?

Unless you want to put down wood chips, the answer is yes. However, don't be too quick to dismiss the wood chip option. It can be really practical, especially if you already own a petting zoo. Babies are cute, and if you've already got some little goats and pigs and stuff, adding an infant to your petting zoo could make it a real winner. Who knows? Maybe you'll win some sort of petting-zoo innovation award before the government comes to take away your baby. Good luck!

For the rest of us, there are two diapering options.

Cloth or Disposable?

Scientists tell us that, if trends continue, the world will be completely full of disposable diapers by 2070. This raises two points: (a) by 2070 you'll likely be dead, and – ironically – your kid will have to deal with it; and (b) maybe getting entirely filled with diapers is exactly what happened to the World of Diapering and that's how the place got its name.

Should you be concerned about the environmental impact of disposable diapers? By using the most convenient option, are we consigning our children to some sort of nightmarish, diaper-apocalyptic Mad Max-type of future, where diaper is king and man is slave? And if so will this future be cool and exciting like *Mad Max* or lame and boring like *Mad Max Beyond Thunderdome*? The answer is left to the reader.

Instead of choosing between cloth and disposable, the option is to buy cloth diapers and then dispose of them. The route is most often taken by wealthy parents who want to be environmentally friendly but then chicken out when they realize they have to wash all those dirty diapers.

Premium or Generic?
If you choose disposable diapers, you'll find yourself faced with a bewildering array of brands and options. You may wish to try them all and see which you prefer. However, they probably won't fit you because they're made for babies.

Name-brand and generic diapers may seem similar, but in fact they are different in many ways. For example, some of the premium brands are scented to smell like baby powder. Also, some name brand diapers offer incentives, such as "diaper points." Simply buy more diapers to collect more points. Trade them in for great rewards. Combine them with your Air Miles to go on long flights where nobody has to get up to go to the bathroom because everybody's wearing diapers. It's so much fun that you'll want to keep buying diapers well into your child's college years.

You real choice among disposable diapers is a matter of Muppets. On the front of every one there's a little strip of Velcro-like material. Usually, this strip features a little cartoon decoration. Sometimes it's a dog or a clown, but usually, it's a Muppet.

Is the diaper a low-end department store brand? It's got a Muppet. Is it a deluxe premium brand? It's got a Muppet. Did you buy it in a remote village in the middle of the rain forest that you visited while travelling around the world using your diaper points? It's got a Muppet.

Somehow the Muppet people have made separate deals with every known diaper manufacturer. The price of the diaper determines whether or not you get an A-list Muppet. A no-name brand might have some sort of blue furry thing you vaguely remember from your own childhood. A mid-range diaper might give you Ernie or Bert. If you've really broken the bank, your diaper might feature Elmo.

Why are the Muppets kings of diaper product placement? Why are the strips decorated anyway? It's not for the baby's benefit – a baby can't see his own diaper, unless he's got a mirror over his change table like a miniature Hugh Hefner.

Really, the only person who sees the diaper strip is the parent, while changing the diaper. That's why the Muppets should be replaced by something aimed at adults, like recent baseball scores or maybe a Far Side cartoon.

If you still can't decide which brand to buy, pay attention to TV commercials. At their best, diaper ads come pretty close to making almost no sense at all. You've likely tuned them out until this point in your life, but now that you're in the target audience, have a look.

They're sickeningly cute and sweet and just plain *weird*, with computer-animated babies walking around and dancing and lip-synching and talking to computer-animated gnomes and opening treasure chests and flying in space with weird computer-animated glittering stars and other computer-animated strangeness. They seem to be designed by, and aimed at, people on drugs.

Are stoned people big diaper buyers? No. But new parents are, and due to lack of sleep new parents are basically stoned and therefore attracted to glittering computer-animated babies floating with gnomes in space.

In fact, psychedelic diaper commercials are a sound advertising strategy. Or would be, if new parents had time to watch TV.

Scott

You'd be hard-pressed to formulate a substantial grievance with human evolution. I mean, here we are, on a planet that's rotating at some absurd speed while following an orbit at an even more absurd speed around a gigantic celestial gas ball in some cute little solar system that's part of a massive galaxy that barely qualifies as a speck of dust in the context of the universe and yet nature has still had the foresight to outfit us with what amounts to a backup kidney, in case a loved one requires a transplant, or we find ourselves in desperate need of a couple thousand bucks. Plus, ours is, to my knowledge, the only species on Earth that can open bottlecaps with its teeth. Take that, muskox!

Still, every once in a while, some singular aspect of the human animal makes me believe that something out there – Nature, God, Tom Green – has the most twisted sense of humour. Bald men with lush, thick beards come to mind. Bald women with lush, thick beards come to mind, too, though strangely only when I'm fantasizing. My point is this: How could Darwin's theory of natural selection be afforded any credence whatsoever when large swaths of the allegedly dominant human race continue to carry the precise genetic coding required to grow a mullet?

When my first son was born, I found myself unable to resist the urge to count his fingers and toes. For this, and for my crack addiction, my fondness for loose women, and my possession of Journey's *Greatest Hits*, I blame society – and, to a lesser extent, the damnably intoxicating vocal stylings of Mr. Steve Perry. The presence of ten fingers and ten toes at some point in human existence became synonymous with a healthy baby. Ten fingers? Ten toes? Healthy baby. Personally, if it had been up to me to create a counting-related synonym for a healthy baby, I might have started with, say, the head. One head? Healthy baby. But heads don't take that long to count, and let's be honest – this whole finger-and-toe-counting thing was probably just invented to give new fathers something to do besides looking ashen and mumbling incoherently.

So I counted the toes and I counted the fingers and that's when I noticed them. The fingernails. My son had emerged from the womb and navigated the birth canal with ten adorable little fingers and ten perfectly formed little fingernails – that could slice their way through sheet metal. These things were long and they were *sharp*. I couldn't help but ask myself some questions: Why does a baby need long, sharp fingernails? What in the history of the human species has compelled our innate sensibilities to evolve our physical characteristics to the point that some children emerge from the womb just a spandex suit and a couple lamb-chop sideburns away from being able to venture out on Halloween as Wolverine? Also, who actually eats at Red Lobster?

Confronted with my darling child's talons, my first instinct, as it is whenever I am presented with a problem or task or challenge, was to ignore it in the hopes that it would Go Away. Alas, barely twelve hours into his life, James had succeeded in using his fingernails and his inherent newborn spasticity to inflict a comprehensive pattern of angry red slashes across his face. Clearly, the nails would have to be trimmed. Or the face would need to be coated in some thick, protective shellac. And I'm a real klutz when it comes to woodworking.

I picked up the baby nail clippers.

You know how every so often there's a story in the local paper about some guy who carved, like, two hundred and eighty-three angels onto the pit of a cherry? Next time you see that story, write down the guy's name. Look up his phone number and get in touch. This is the guy who should be trimming your newborn's fingernails. Why? Have you ever looked at a baby's fingers? They're small, really small. Which means the nails on those fingers are, in most cases, even smaller. So what you end up with is (a) a nervous new parent, (b) a sharp cutting implement, and (c) a defenceless baby prone to sudden jerky movements. This is quite possibly the least advisable combination of elements since (a) a ten-dollar movie ticket, (b) a darkened theatre, and (c) *The Postman*.

As a public service, I present the results of the inaugural trimming of the five nails on the right hand of my infant son. Think of it this way: You can't possibly do any worse.

1. Snip. *Wahhh!* Blood. Abject apologies. Declaration of inability to carry on. General feeling of all-round worthlessness as a human being and a parent.

2. Snip. *Wahhh!* More blood. Abjecter apologies. Beads of sweat forming on brow. Hands shaking noticeably.

3. Snip. Silence. No blood.

4. Snip. Silence. No blood. Woo-hoo! I am the king of the –

5. Snip. *Wahhh!* Blood. Abjectest apologies. Sweat wiped from forehead with shirt sleeve. Eyes turn to doorway to catch expected entry of stern-faced caseworkers from social services armed with court-order custody papers and a Taser. Handing off of clippers to child's mother to do other hand.

RESUMING SEXUAL RELATIONS
AFTER THE BIRTH OF YOUR CHILD

As if.

As a new parent, you will already be acutely aware that the process of conceiving, carrying, and giving birth to a child is rife with social ritual. First, you tell everyone that you're going to have a baby. Then you tell everyone every day how the pregnancy is going. Then you attend a baby shower and tell your senile, inebriated aunt that you really appreciate her thoughtful gift of Baby's First Nail Gun. Finally, mercifully, you tell everyone the baby has been born. (Many scientists now believe that the human gestation period of nine months was established not because of biological demands but rather because it is the maximum amount of time a woman can endure hearing the remark "You're getting *so* big!" without jamming her fist into the person's cakehole.)

It is important for you to be aware that the birth of your child does not mean the end of the social ritual. There is still one last mandatory ceremonial function associated with the arrival in the world of a brand-new human being. Well, two, if you count the "ceremonial" freaking out over the realization that you're actually responsible for the actual well-being of a real, live person. But the function we're talking about is the Baby Reveal.

Short of leaving town or constantly playing the CDs of Kathie Lee Gifford, there is no way to avoid it: people will be coming over to your home to see your baby. In fact, people may be over right now. They may even have brought you this book as a gift both to celebrate the birth of your child and subtly mock your apparent lack of parenting skills. Bunch of smartasses is what they are. But smartasses with excellent taste in the selection of parental advice literature.

Our point is this: Seeing the baby is a big deal. There are conversations about seeing the baby. Appointments are made to see the baby. Gifts are purchased to be given on the occasion of seeing the baby. And shareholders in Gap Inc. are amazed and appreciative that someone actually spent $140 on a tiny cashmere sweater that the baby will wear for as many as five minutes before soiling or, more likely, outgrowing.

But the thing about seeing the baby is that seeing the baby is not, if you think about it, a particularly time-consuming chore. In fact, top researchers have found that, technically speaking, it takes only a fraction of a second to actually *see* the baby, and perhaps a few nanoseconds longer to see twins. Seeing triplets, by way of comparison, takes a full five to seven seconds, but that's because the visiting couple will spend four of those seconds looking at each other and making facial expressions that efficiently convey the sentiment, "Triplets! Thank God this isn't us!"

Let us emphasize: We are not suggesting that the typical Baby Reveal lasts for only a fraction of a second. To the contrary, most people will pretend to be interested in looking at your baby for as long as thirty whole seconds. *Look, there he is – the baby! We've come to see the baby and there it is being seen. Yup, that's definitely a baby. A baby that's lying there and not doing all that much, except being seen. Hmmm . . . I wonder if the Red Sox are winning. That's a baby, all right. Did I leave the iron plugged in? Cute baby. Spider-Man, Spider-Man/Does whatever a spider can . . .*

You will, as a new parent, swiftly discover that an integral part of the Baby Reveal is talking about the baby that's being revealed. The baby can't talk and, as the baby's parents, you'll be too fatigued to communicate in anything other than grunts, gestures, and perhaps some meaningful drooling. This leaves your guests to do most of the talking. Here's a handy guide to what they'll be trying to tell you:

What They Say and What They Mean
• *He's so cute!* He's immobile and sleeping and devoid of any perceptible qualities.
• *He's absolutely adorable!* He's immobile and sleeping and devoid of any perceptible qualities.
• *What a cute baby!* He's immobile and sleeping and devoid of any perceptible qualities.
• *He looks just like you!* He's immobile and sleeping and devoid of any perceptible qualities.
• *Did I mention how cute he is?* He's immobile and sleeping and devoid of any perceptible qualities.
• *[Awkward silence]* He's immobile and sleeping and devoid of any perceptible qualities.
• *What a perfect little angel!* He's immobile and sleeping and devoid of any perceptible qualities.
• *Wow, that sure is one cute baby!* Are you going to make me stand here all day or are you finally going to offer me a beer or something?

The protocol of this type of visit demands that the Baby Reveal and talking while the baby is revealed be followed by much discussion about having seen the baby. Questions are asked. Answers are given. Yawns are suppressed.

This is the point at which we should probably mention a universal truth: Everyone who comes to see the baby will, mere minutes after arriving, be desperate to get out of your house. We are not kidding. If you doubt us, just look at the facts for yourself. Your baby is not good company: he just lies there looking all spaced out and clueless. You and your spouse are not good company: you just lie there looking all spaced out and clueless. You used to talk about current events and gossip and sex and work and lawn care and movies and clothes and foreign affairs and jazz. Now you pretty much talk exclusively about infant feces and where you stand on the pressing question of Pampers versus Huggies. It will take about five minutes for anyone who visits you to wish they were instead catching the Pauly Shore triple bill in the seventh circle of Hell.

What can you do to make the ritual of the Baby Reveal more palatable and enjoyable for those who come to visit? Nothing. And frankly we wouldn't even bother trying. If people are coming to visit you, that means they at least got to go outside for a minute or two, which is more than you've managed. So make those lucky bastards suffer. Show them the 487 photos you've taken of the first seventy-two hours of your baby's life. Subject them to rambling meditations of how best to encourage "latching" during breast-feeding. Repeatedly utter the word "poop." And then try to stifle your hoots of laughter as your visitors squirm, check their watches, and silently pray for a swift and merciful death.

You're a parent now: The opportunities for "fun" will be few and far between. You can't afford to waste one.

Let's face it: no matter how dedicated a parent you are, you can't be everywhere. And when we say "everywhere" we mean you can't be in your baby's room, in your house, only feet away from your own bedroom. And when we say "can't" we mean "don't want to."

Luckily for you there's such a thing as a baby monitor.

What Is a Baby Monitor?

A baby monitor is actually a set of two radio transmitters. One is placed in the baby's room, where it is able to listen in on your baby's activities, while the other goes with you to the bar.

No! Not to the bar! That's not responsible. Besides, everybody at the bar would make fun of you for having this baby monitor stuck on your belt. And what if instead of bringing the receiver, you accidentally brought the transmitter to the bar? Now your baby can hear *you*, drunk, getting into an argument with some guy about who was the best member of the A-Team. Which is stupid, because we all know it's Face.

No, you won't be using your baby monitor to go drinking at some bar. Instead, you'll be using it within your own home, to listen in on your sleeping child while you perform other activities. Such as drinking alone in the kitchen.

Types of Monitors

Audio monitors are the most basic type of baby monitor. Actually, a more basic type of baby monitor is the now-rare telegraph monitor. However, this requires the baby to learn Morse code, something many children don't master until they're at least three. The telegraph monitor replaced the even more basic carrier pigeon and smoke signal styles of baby monitor.

Audio monitors come with a number of options. Sound and light monitors feature a series of blinking lights. When your baby starts to cry, the blinking lights blink. The idea here is if you're working in a noisy environment, or if you're sitting around listening to recordings of babies crying, and your real baby actually starts to cry, you'll see the blinking and act appropriately.

The downside is if your baby starts really wailing those lights will start blinking so much that you might have a seizure. This is why you should purchase a second baby monitor to monitor yourself and give the receiver to *your* parents, who will then be able to come over and slip a wallet between your teeth so you don't swallow your tongue. Then, assuming you survive, and since your folks are there anyway, you can con them into doing some babysitting while you go to the bar. Plus you kept the wallet. Perfect!

Another kind is the intercom monitor which also functions as an intercom. For example, while up in your baby's room you might send a message to your spouse: "Why am I up here in the baby's room while you get to sit down there eating multiple canisters of Pringles?" Your spouse then has the option of pushing a button on the receiver saying he's coming right up to help. Or, more likely, he could not push that button.

Or, if he's smart, he'll do that old trick from World War Two movies, where you make static noises with your mouth and send back a message like: "Command, your transmission is garbled, can't receive your new orders, will continue to eat Pringles canisters until supplies run out. Over."

Note that baby monitors may have multiple features, such as a monitor that has both an intercom and blinking lights. This can be useful because if your spouse uses it to talk to you, you don't have to listen – you can just wait for the lights to stop blinking before grunting noncommittally. This can save your relationship.

Video monitors are a step up from audio-only monitors. They incorporate a video camera that allows you not only to hear but also *see* your sleeping infant. You can spend hours watching a blurry black-and-white picture of your little baby, lying there in bed, sleeping, not doing anything. Surprisingly, this will often be better than what's on TV.

But, if not, point the remote control at it so you can flip around and see what other people's kids are doing. Now *that's* TV! Too bad your spouse ate all the Pringles.

Some video baby monitors utilize infrared technology so you can see your baby on the screen even if the nursery is completely dark. Get the one that comes with a pair of scissors so that you can cut out a picture of your baby and tape it to the screen. Now you can see your baby on the screen even if the nursery is completely dark and your baby isn't in the nursery because she's sitting right there with you. Some monitors may even allow you to smell your baby from a hundred feet away. Who knows? Science marches on!

What product is right for you? How much surveillance is too much? If, when your toddler is playing with his little friends, he points at the monitor and mouths the words, "It's not safe here" and then turns on some loud music before talking in hushed whispers in the corner, you may have overdone it. On the other hand, what are those kids up to? Two-year-olds can be pretty shifty. See if you can cut a deal with one of the smaller kids to turn rat.

Are Baby Monitors Safe?
Some parents have concerns that baby monitors and other wireless electronic equipment may pose a health risk, similar to the potential health risks posed by cellphones. Although there is no scientific evidence for such a concern, experts do agree that, like cellphones, baby monitors should never be used while your infant is driving.

If you are worried about using an electronic baby monitor, there are more low-tech alternatives.

Cut a Hole in the Wall
This allows you to see, hear, smell, touch, poke with a stick, and otherwise interact with your infant. Note that you may have to cut through several walls, depending where you are in your house. Also note that the sound of the chainsaw may interfere with your child's sleeping.

Hire a Guy

With the fall of the Soviet Union, there are many former KGB surveillance experts who are now working freelance on the open market. Hiring one to tail your infant will give you peace of mind, and – taking into account the exchange rate – may actually be cheaper than a baby monitor. Drawbacks: as your child gets older and becomes more independent he may try to "shake" his tail, prompting exciting stroller chases and gunfights.

Also, what if you toddler "turns" your agent, bribes him, or cajoles him into spying on *you*? Will you use the traitor to feed your child false information? Or will he have an unfortunate "accident"? Experts agree the answer depends on your parenting style.

When Should I Stop Using the Baby Monitor?

Many parents become so accustomed to the baby monitor that they don't know when to stop using it. When does a child become old enough to no longer require this kind of supervision? Experts say a good rule of thumb is this: If you turn on the baby monitor, and you hear the sound of your kid talking to *her* kids, it's time to quit.

Conclusion

A baby monitor can keep your child safe, provide you with some independence and – perhaps most importantly – prepare your child for the nightmarish world of the future where privacy is a thing of the past and Big Brother is always watching.

Why not take our quick quiz to review the information from this section?

Baby Monitor Quick Quiz
1) Who was the best member of the A-Team?
   a) Hannibal
   b) Face
   c) B.A. Barracus
   d) Mad Murdock

Answer: B.

Your relationship with your child will lead to many memorable moments, events that will stay vivid in your mind, replaying themselves over and over in your head for the rest of your life.

There will also be some *good* memories, but you'll tend to forget those. So maybe you'll want to take some pictures or something. The question is, what with?

Camera

Well, chances are you own a camera. But whereas before it may have just sat in a closet collecting dust during the long months between summer holidays and Christmas, *now* you've actually got something to take pictures of year round. A baby.

Let's face it, nobody wants to look at pictures of *you* (unless you're a supermodel or something). Even *you* don't want to look at pictures of you (unless you're a vain supermodel or something). No, people would much rather look at a picture of a baby. A cute little gurgling baby. First he's lying on a blanket. Then he's lying in the car seat. Then he's lying on a blanket. Look: he's wearing a different shirt! Only thirty-three pictures left to go.

Okay, so grandparents aside, people *don't* want to look at pictures of your baby. But you'll want to take them anyway.

And for that, you'll have to dust off that camera you already own. Or maybe you'll start hankering for a new one.

Film-Based Cameras

Before there were digital cameras, there were film cameras. Actually, before there were digital cameras there were a lot of things: oil paintings, Zeppelins, the Spanish Inquisition. Most of History came before digital cameras. But let's concentrate on film cameras for now.

Film offers a number of advantages and disadvantages compared to digital imaging. You have to take the film in to get it processed. This can be a problem for a new parent, because it can be hard to find the time. Film rolls tend to pile up and the next thing you know you're asking your kid to drop off the rolls of baby pictures on his way to college. On the other hand, film cameras are cheaper than digital cameras. Plus you don't need to own a computer to use one. Plus if you live in Most of History digital cameras aren't invented yet, so you'll have to use a film camera to take pictures of the Spanish Inquisition as you float past in your Zeppelin.

Digital Cameras

Digital cameras are the new cool thing! You have *got* to get one of these things! We're serious, you've *got* to!

Have you gotten one yet? No? You disgust us.

A digital photography system will allow you to take photos using your digital camera, then load them onto your digital home computer, and edit them using your digital photography software, which can be controlled by your digital mouse-pointing device that is manipulated by your fingers, also known as digits.

What kind of things can you do with a computer and a camera? Well, you can remove blemishes, such as the ones that form on your face when you spend long hours sitting in front of a computer editing digital photos and eating junk food. Or you can remove "red-eye." Red-eye is a red tint that might appear in the corneas of your child's eyes in a photo. This happens for one of two reasons:

1. The camera's flash is too close to the child. Back away slightly.

2. Your child is Satan. Back away even farther.

You can also use a digital camera to post your child's picture on the Internet so that friends and relatives who live far away can lie and say they looked at it.

Camcorder

There are a lot of fun, action-packed moments in children's lives. Times when they're being really cute or doing something adorable that just wouldn't come across in a photo. If your kids are doing something like this, and you want them to stop immediately, pull out a camcorder.

Remember that *Looney Tunes* cartoon with the singing frog? It would do this amazing song and dance routine until someone was looking and then, nothing. The same principle applies to your kids. By the time you can find the camcorder, pull it out of the overpriced camcorder bag you bought, take off the lens cap, point it at them, and hit Record, they're done doing whatever it was that was cute. *Riiiibiiiit.*

However, a camcorder is still a great purchase. For years to come you'll be able to savour many fabulous moments as you watch hours of footage of kids who just recently finished doing something cute.

Taking Better Pictures of Your Kids

Now that you've got the equipment all you need is the know-how. How to take better pictures of your kids could be a book in itself. Maybe not a very good book – not unless the author at least throws in some anecdotes and whatnot – but a book nevertheless.

Here are some time-tested techniques that will improve your family snaps.

Be patient. Don't expect to get the perfect shot in the first few seconds. Have your camera ready and wait. It may be a few moments before your child makes the perfect face or strikes the perfect pose for a truly outstanding picture. Or you might have to wait longer. Your child may grow up and you might have to have another child as you hold your camera, waiting, always waiting.

Eventually you will grow old and realize you've wasted your whole life sitting there holding a camera. But at this point don't put the camera down. You've already wasted your life so you might as well get this picture – *and it better be a good one!*

Shoot at eye level. Amateur photographers often make the mistake of shooting their subjects from an odd angle. Professional photographers often make the mistake of getting too close to Sean Penn and getting punched. Either mistake can be avoided.

Shooting your toddler from your full height will exaggerate the size of his head. If your child has a small head or, alternately, a large body, then go for it. Or if the person you're going to show the photo to has an unusually large head, and you want them to feel comfortable and like your child because you're in their will or something, then by all means go for the monster head-shot.

Otherwise, crouch down and shoot your child from her own level. It'll make a better picture and, who knows, it might do you some good to look at things from this angle. After all, this is how she sees the world. Except for the white box floating in mid-air. That's from the viewfinder, you idiot.

Get close. Try to fill the frame with your subject. Often, parents make the mistake of sending their kids off to pose next to some large object such as a sign saying "Welcome to Glendon, Alberta, Home of the World's Largest Perogy," and then taking their picture from fifty feet away. This is a mistake – both to travel to Glendon to see a big fibreglass dumpling and to take a photo from such a distance.

Get close to your kids. Then use your camera's zoom to get even closer. Look through the viewfinder. Do you like what you see? No? Then go find some better-looking kids and take a picture of them.

Place your subject off-centre. Putting your subject directly in the middle of the frame is boring. Yes, your kid is just sitting there in the high chair watching *Bob the Builder*, and we all know that's boring anyway, but these are the relatively golden moments and we have to make the best of them.

Placing your kids towards one side of the frame can make a photo more dynamic. This is called *composition* and is part of a long tradition in human history known as *art*. If you'd spent more time in museums instead of travelling to Glendon to see giant perogies you would already know this.

Conclusion

Recording your first months as a parent can be difficult, but it's well worth the effort. In years to come this photographic record will provide hours of enjoyment and, perhaps more importantly, vital documentation for any future legal action.

Unless your obstetrician is very skilled, and a bit of a show-off, your baby will be born naked. There's no shame in this.

You may think it's necessary to provide your newborn child with clothing. In fact, it isn't – that's what grandparents are for. Baby clothing bought by a grandparent is just like any other kind of baby clothing, except for two key differences:

1. Quantity. Grandparent-purchased baby clothing keeps showing up at your house at an exponentially increasing rate, until the birth of a second child, at which point it suddenly stops.

2. Price. The average price of an item of grandparent-purchased baby clothing is, approximately, a million billion dollars.

Grandparents shop for baby clothes at different stores than parents do. While a parent might buy a little shirt or sleeper from a department store or a discount rack, grandparents buy baby clothing at special expensive just-for-grandparent baby shops with names like "Saw You Coming."

A parent-bought baby outfit is simple, just enough to provide warmth and protection from the environment. A grandparent-bought baby outfit is a multi-layered, multi-part ensemble consisting of a button-down shirt, pants (with real pockets so the baby can carry his credit cards and keys), a vest, matching socks, a hat, and, possibly, cufflinks – the entire ensemble exactly like something from the runways of Paris, except perfectly scaled down. Like a model railroad of clothing.

In spite of all the expense and the trouble, a grandparent-bought baby outfit is a good purchase. It's made from high-quality materials designed to survive years of use, if for some reason your baby doesn't grow and stays exactly the same size. If you've got the growing type of baby, you better start suiting the kid up now because he'll probably outgrow the outfit before you can get the cufflinks on.

You can't rely on grandparents for all the clothes you'll need; it may mean visiting them every week. Sooner or later, you'll have to learn baby fashion basics:

The Onesie

The onesie is a simple T-shirt-style garment. It's typically short-sleeved, has snaps at the crotch to provide easy access to the diaper, and, for some reason, makes your baby look like a cast member from an early episode of *Star Trek*.

Seriously. It's hilarious. They're almost always primary colours, all they need is a little *Star Trek* badge over the left breast and your baby would be all set. Or maybe epaulettes for a more *Forbidden Planet*-type look. Either way, they have a definite science-fictiony quality to them.

This makes sense if you think about it. Science fiction people are people from the future, and people from the future are, presumably, babies now. So apparently onesies look like sci-fi jumpsuits because sci-fi jumpsuits actually *are* onesies that the future people scaled up because they liked them so much when they were babies.

Leggings

Baby girls wear leggings, baby boys wear pants. Or, rather, parents of baby girls try to make them wear leggings, and parents of baby boys try to make them wear pants.

You've heard the expression "we all put on our pants one leg at a time." Except for babies. Babies put their pants on no legs at a time. They lie on their back and kick at you with a preternatural, apparently instinctive ability to hamper any attempt at getting their legs into the pants.

Here's how to put pants on a baby:

1. Lay baby on back.

2. Put hand up into right pant leg, grab right foot, pull foot through right pant leg.

3. Put other hand into left pant leg, grab left foot.

4. Baby removes right leg from right pant leg.

5. While still holding onto left foot, put other hand into right pant leg and attempt to grab right foot.

6. Baby removes left leg from left pant leg.

7. Buy a kilt.

Hats

If you grew up in the 1970s, you might remember being told to go outside and play. This is because people at the time for some reason laboured under the delusion that sunshine and fresh air are good for you. We now know this to be false. Sunshine is a deadly, deadly poison and eventually they'll probably figure out air is bad for you too.

That the rays of the sun are deadly shouldn't be a surprise to anyone, considering that the sun is basically a giant nuclear reactor hovering in space. Eventually, activists will probably succeed in getting it shut down, but until then our children must wear hats.

When choosing a child's sun hat, make sure you pick something that's light, comfortable, and has a wide brim to provide full coverage. Pick a hat that's several sizes too big, to allow the skull to continue growing after you Krazy Glue it onto the kid's head, because that's the only way you'll get her to wear it.

Shoes

It's possible to buy sneakers, sandals, and even dress shoes in tiny sizes for newborn babies. Many of these will end up being bronzed and kept as keepsakes, and in fact if you're buying a pair you might as well get them bronzed and mounted at the point-of-purchase because, of course, bronzed or not, they're totally useless.

The problem with shoes for newborns is technical, but in simplified layman's terms it boils down to this: *babies can't walk*. Therefore, the whole shoe thing is a waste of time.

Older children who do walk may appreciate owning shoes, especially because, in combination with shirts, they allow one to get service.

Pyjamas

For some reason, children are expected to wear pyjamas, even though most adults don't. Those adults who *do* wear pyjamas wear them all the time and never take them off (for example, Hugh Hefner).

Why is it that children are required to wear pyjamas but are prohibited from having a smoking jacket and a pipe and going to late-night parties with supermodels? No one knows. But the good news is baby pyjamas look even more like *Star Trek* outfits than onesies do, so enjoy.

Miscellaneous: Jackets, Boots, Sweaters, Etc.

Yeah, you have to buy these too.

SIGNS YOU MAY HAVE PICKED THE WRONG PEDIATRICIAN

- He almost strangles himself while attempting to remove the stethoscope from around his neck.
- Diploma is always "at the cleaners."
- Tongue depressor tastes suspiciously like a Creamsicle.
- Before beginning routine checkup of your child, *he* strips.
- Colleagues greet him with enthusiastic "Hi, Dr. Nick!"
- Other people in waiting room are all holding sick pets.
- Arrives for emergency house call in ice-cream truck.
- Claims to be able to gauge child's heart rate using her "magic glasses."
- Pocket of white coat bears logo of local supermarket's meat department.
- You notice she only diagnoses your baby with ailments that were recently featured on *E.R.*
- The "X-Ray Machine" is a piece of plywood with a skeleton painted on it.
- Keeps asking if you'd like fries with your inoculations.
- Consults anatomical text and then shouts: "Oh, right, the *arm*. I always forget that one!"
- Leaves in middle of ear exam to deliver pizza.
- So-called nurse appears to be same person wearing a wig.
- Just before he enters the examination room to care for your precious, precious child, you notice him cracking a beer.

Inspired by the U.S. government's colour-coded assessment of the current terrorist threat level, we have devised a similar system to help new parents accurately gauge the prevailing dangers to their sanity. We recommend that you keep the current Parental Threat Level posted in a place where it is likely to be seen for a few minutes during each twenty-four-hour period. The back of your eyelids, for instance. They should be closed about that long.

Green (Low Risk): Child sleeping contentedly. House sparkling clean. Birds chirping serenely on windowsill as parents conclude leisurely lovemaking session and commence baking an apple pie from scratch while holding hands.

Blue (General Risk): Child awake. House in moderate disarray. One parent sleep-deprived. The other parent sleeping contentedly, but sadly it's at his office desk. Birds defecating serenely on windowsill.

Yellow (Elevated Risk): Child crying. House filthy. Parents, between shots of peach schnapps, wax nostalgic over halcyon, pre-child days and drunkenly agree to legally change child's middle name to The Plague.

Orange (High Risk): Child bawling *and* whining. House strewn with toys, clothes, and empty peach schnapps bottles. Carcasses of birds on windowsill being pecked at by rabid vultures. Parents are urged to watch closely for suspicious behaviour, such as your spouse packing three or more suitcases of clothing for alleged trip to "corner store."

Red (Severe Risk): Child's head rotating a minimum of 360 degrees. Priest screaming: "The power of Christ compels you!" House bleeding.

Scott

In the course of raising your child, you will at one time or another come to believe you are doing everything wrong. There is a simple explanation for this: You *are* doing everything wrong. Then again, there is a very good chance you are doing everything right. It all depends which parental advice book is sitting dog-eared, coffee-stained, and pea-covered on the bookshelf.

Is there any aspect of the human experience that attracts advice in the same enthusiastic quantities as parenting? Fine, golf. But apart from that. Friends are only too willing to impart tremendous morsels of child-rearing wisdom; strangers, too, for that matter. Grandparents tend to convey their counsel through quiet, but not so quiet that you can't hear them, tuts and sighs. Eye-rolling, too. Eye-rolling is very big with grandparents. Only rarely will any of these advisers actually wait for you to ask for their advice. Weirder still, they won't stop dispensing advice, even after you subtly make clear that you don't want their advice by subtly hollering, "I don't want your advice!"

Books have the mitigating quality of not being able to shout advice at you across the dinner table, but that does not mean that reading their pages will be any less maddening. At least, not if you happen to consult more than one. In many cases, the authors' advice – usually presented within each book as the best and only way to go – will be profoundly contradictory. Consider, for example, the contentious business of nighttime crying and how to respond to it. Some parents swear by the notion of letting their baby wail away in the hopes he'll swiftly figure out how to fall asleep without help. Others contend this tactic borders on child abuse and instead spend hours back rubbing their bawling babies. What do the experts say? Well, the experts say it's crazy to let your kids howl all night. Except, that is, for those experts who say it's not crazy at all.

"If your toddler cries, it is probably best not to let too much time elapse before going to comfort him," instructs *The Yale Child Study Center Guide to Understanding Your Child*. Lee Salk, quoted in *The Happiest Baby on the Block*, is more emphatic: "Crying is good for the lungs the way bleeding is good for the veins." And author Harvey Karp concurs: "Letting your baby cry it out makes as little sense as closing your ears to your screeching car alarm while you wait for the battery to die."

But then there are the people behind *What to Expect the First Year*, one of the volumes in the wildly popular series of advice manuals. They opine: "'Crying it out' may indeed seem cruel and inhuman punishment, especially when his only crime is wanting Mommy or Daddy in the middle of the night. But it is actually the best way, sleep experts tell us, to respond to a baby's need to learn how to fall asleep on his own." And *The Gift of Good Manners* adds: "As difficult as it is to hear a baby cry for even a short time, the delay can be an important first step toward the development of a considerate child."

And then there is the pacifier. Readers of *The Happiest Baby on the Block* will emerge of the mind that pacifiers are a useful tool. "Sucking is the icing on the cake of calming," the book decrees. "It takes a baby who is beginning to quiet and lulls him into a deep and profound state of tranquility." Meantime, the *New Mother's Guide to Breastfeeding* declares: "Do not allow your newborn to be given a pacifier. Ask your obstetrician or pediatrician to write an order to this effect if needed." Even a hurried reading of the bold declarations of these self-proclaimed experts will lead a sensible person to conclude that the authors who provide the fewest useful tips are those who claim to have all the answers.

Shortly after my son James turned two, I watched for the first time a parenting program on television. I came across it just as it was starting. It was called "Mindful Parenting" and it was hosted by Jon Kabat-Zinn, who was introduced as the founder and director of the Stress Reduction Clinic at the University of Massachusetts Medical Center. He was wearing a cuddly sweater. This got me to thinking that it was probably a prerequisite of his job that he dress himself in a cuddly sweater and speak in a placid tone that suggests Perry Como on a Valium bender. No matter her academic credentials, Joan Rivers could never direct the Stress Reduction Clinic at the University of Massachusetts Medical Center.

When first we glimpsed Kabat-Zinn, he was gesturing serenely from a stress-free armchair, which was positioned in front of a calm lamp and a tranquil window that revealed a bucolic snowfall. Somewhere, a peaceful piano tinkled softly. He had yet to complete a sentence, and already Kabat-Zinn's secret to effective parenting had been made clear: Force your kids to watch this show. It's a human tranquilizer.

Kabat-Zinn continued talking serenely. He described the practice of "mindfulness," a philosophical approach that's based on what he described as the non-judgmental, moment-to-moment awareness of your children. Pay attention to your kids, he said. Be kind. Respect their dignity. A dutiful parent myself, I began taking copious notes: Paying attention, eh? And being kind? And respecting their dignity, too? I sat back and silently lamented, "Wow, have I ever been off the mark with my 'mindless' approach of not paying attention, being cruel, and treating my son like a garden gnome." (I'm exaggerating, of course. The fact is I always treat my children with the same respect I'd confer on, say, a lawn jockey.)

Kabat-Zinn made peaceful, stress-free sense at times, but there was something disagreeable about the manner in which he lectured from his Armchair of Serenity, claiming to be a sagacious guide to an experience that, while undeniably universal in nature, is also resoundingly singular in practice. These days, so-called experts abound across the television dial, telling us how best to lose weight and gain self-confidence and apply decorative paint to wicker furniture, how to vote and how to dress and how to dress while voting, how to be the perfect host and the perfect spouse and the perfect parent. But enlightened parenting is, I think most would agree, a tad more complicated and elusive than sprucing up your wicker. You can't just decree: Sand, prime, paint. It's one thing to offer a few clever tips in the hopes they might have some helpful effect. It's rather another to claim to have found "the key to parenting," especially when so many elements of your theory are obvious even to parents in the animal kingdom, most of whom don't get basic cable.

Consider the following utterance, which came as Kabat-Zinn sedately scolded parents for coming home from work and bitching about being tired: "What are our priorities? Why have children? Who are these people? Don't they merit some degree of our energy and at least as much as we're devoting to our work?" In academe, this is known as the Duh phase of a thesis, the point at which the insultingly evident is stated in order to prepare folks for the ensuing brainy observations. Kabat-Zinn continued: "But how do you actually do that? It's a huge question, juggling work and family. It's unspeakably huge. But we need to ask ourselves: 'What are we doing? What's important here?'" And then, having answered his five big questions with two bigger questions, he and his cuddly sweater moved on.

Posing difficult queries is easy. Providing insightful, persuasive answers is not. Watch, I'll prove it. Question: How did this guy get to be the focus of an hour-long documentary on his supposedly revolutionary technique of parenting? Answer: Um, beats me.

Paul

Now that the initial rush of having a new baby has ended, and you have time to take stock of the situation, you might look down at your body and fail to recognize yourself. Your pelvis is sore. Your breasts are swollen and tender. Your belly is flabby and distended. Your wife may have similar symptoms.

Let's face it: You need to get into shape. But does your new role as parent mean you won't have time to take care of yourself? Yes, in reality it probably does. But let's pretend it doesn't and see where that takes us. After all, just thinking about exercise must burn *some* calories. Actually, thinking about anything burns calories. So let's think about cake. That's a lot more pleasant.

Are you done yet?

Okay. Back to exercise.

The Gym

Yes, being a parent means it can be hard to get to the gym, or the rock-climbing wall, or the even more advanced rock-climbing wall where people throw rocks at you from the top of the wall, simulating an avalanche.

Many fitness centres do offer babysitting services where you can drop off your children. Unfortunately, you're then supposed to go work out. You can't just drop off the kids and then go eat that cake you've been thinking about for the last few paragraphs.

Another option is to bring your baby with you into the gym. You can carry your infant in a Snugli while you work out. This has the added advantage of being extra ballast, improving your workout. Plus, the people at the top of the avalanche wall will throw fewer rocks at you because they don't want to hit a little baby.

Pilates

Pilates is an exercise program that's easy, effective, and can be performed at home. Plus it's fun!

Okay, it's not fun. Exercise isn't fun. If it was fun, it wouldn't be called "exercise." If sitting watching a Pilates video was fun, then Pilates videos would be released to big-screen theatres and millions of people would line up to see movie stars squatting on big inflatable balls and holding weird positions and grunting a lot.

Pilates might not be for you. If you have some reservations, consider Pilate. Pilate is like Pilates but there's only one of them. Instead of holding a position and breathing, you just breathe.

You can still breathe, can't you? If you have trouble, just lie on your back and get your kid to jump up and down on your chest. This should keep you alive until your spouse gets home and calls for an ambulance.

Tae Bo

Tae Bo is the ancient Eastern art of rearranging furniture to create a better "flow" of mystical energy through a living space. Oh, wait, that's feng shui.

Still, rearranging furniture is pretty good exercise, especially if you don't know what you're doing so you have to do it over and over again until you really feel that mystical energy flowing. Plus, as the parent of a small child, you probably have to move furniture around anyway as you look for the missing Bob the Builder doll that is causing your kid to create the "flow" of mystical screaming energy that fills your living space.

Tae Bo, as opposed to feng shui, is high-energy boxing to music. You may already be doing high-energy boxing to music, say if you've ever tried to put an unwilling child in a car seat while the car stereo is blaring Raffi.

You may wish to combine Tae Bo and feng shui. Feng Tae shui Bo is the ancient practice of rearranging furniture to high-energy music while boxing someone. Sounds like a pretty good workout and you're working out *and* redecorating so you're killing two birds with one stone.

That leads us to our next workout program . . .

Killing Birds with Stones

Now, give it a chance. Throwing a rock is good aerobic activity. It can be performed with one hand while the other pushes a baby carriage or attempts to retrieve a penny from your baby's ear canal or picks up another rock to get that other sneaky bird.

Besides those birds have it coming. I saw part of that Alfred Hitchcock movie *The Birds* and let me tell you this: Those birds were up to something.

Jazzercise

Jazzercise combines two worthy pursuits that *everybody* loves – exercise and jazz. What could be better than working up a sweat and huffing and puffing and stretching aching muscles than doing it *while dancing around to a form of music that nobody likes*?

If you decide to join a jazzercise class, bear in mind that the sight of a parent wearing leotards and, probably, big fluffy wristbands is enough to cause serious mental scars. So, while you do it, make sure to put your child in a babysitting facility far, far away, out of sight. For example, if they have a daycare in that NORAD command bunker under that mountain in the Midwest, that would be a good place.

Same goes for line dancing, except obviously substitute "hat" for "wristbands."

The MacGyver Workout

You may not have time to travel to a gym. You may not have time to put down a Pilates mat or pop a Tae-Bo tape into the VCR. If being a parent has you *this* harassed you've got to resign yourself to an improvised exercise program performed using whatever you can get your hands on – the MacGyver workout.

You can grab a couple of milk jugs out of the fridge and use them as weights. Or do chin-ups on the monkey bars while taking your kids to the playground. Or lift, like, rocks.

These ideas are all well and good . . . but they ignore the most elegant and poetic solution to your exercise dilemma. Your children are the reason you can't get to a gym? *Use your children as a gym.*

Often, you have to pick your children up anyway, for example to put them into a high chair or pull them out of the way of an enraged rhino during a trip to the zoo gone horribly wrong. So instead of just picking them up, why not pick them up, put them down, pick them up, put them down again, and so on until you can "feel the burn"? This is good exercise, and confuses the rhino.

Use your imagination: instead of putting your child into a normal swing that's simply tied to a metal bar, why not put him into a special swing attached to a series of ingenious gears and pulleys leading to a workout bench? Then you can lift and lower your child, concentrating on a different muscle group every day, until you have the body of a god or goddess.

(With any luck, if you're a man you'll get the "god" body, and if you're a woman you'll get "goddess," but either way at least now you're in shape.)

Why wimp out and put your child into a high chair, when you can get a better workout by putting him into a *very* high chair? Or an *extremely* high chair, attached to some sort of flywheel that moves it back and forth, providing you with an aerobic workout? No pain, no gain!

And why buy expensive jogging weights that strap to your ankles, when you can strap a pair of infants to your legs? The kids will like it and, if they're identical twins, your legs will get an even workout. If not you'll have to strap kids onto alternate legs on alternate days, or get the smaller kid to hold a friend.

The possibilities are endless. And, best of all, as your body grows stronger and your muscles tone up, your child will grow heavier, providing you with a better workout.

Eventually your child will be twenty and won't want to be strapped to your leg. But at this point you'll be so strong and pumped up that you'll be able to strap anyone you want onto your leg, no questions asked.

At the end of the day, isn't that what it's all about?

Conclusion

You're still thinking about cake, aren't you? Let's face it, you're never working out again, if you even did before the baby was born – which, looking at you, is hard to believe.

If you really wanted to you could have done some quick push-ups in the time you spent reading the last few pages. But you didn't and that's because you are lazy.

You might think I'm using a little reverse psychology, setting a discouraging tone so that you'll go work out just to prove me wrong. If that's what you think, you'd be . . . wrong, fatso!

I really am trying to discourage you. Because if you're not working out, and you're all flabby and unattractive, that lowers the bar for everyone else. And everyone else includes me, and I don't want to work out.

Let's face it, having a young child is a great excuse *not* to go to the gym. Who can blame you? So enjoy, and hope that future medical science will be able to repair the damage you do to yourself today. Maybe some future miniature laser robot will be injected into your arteries to explode that pudding blockage that you're creating every day with your carefree pudding consumption.

On the other hand, maybe scientists will never invent a miniature pudding-busting laser robot. So maybe we shouldn't have pudding. Let's have cake instead.

Okay, you've got a kid now. Your wild days are over. No more partying all night at some crazy dance club. No spontaneous trips to the lake. No more, well, no more leaving the house really.

Actually, that's not true. There will be times when you'll have to leave the house. If the house is on fire, for example. And when these rare occasions come up, you'll have to pack the baby travel kit.

Manoeuvring around on the Earth's surface with a little kid is different from the kind of travel you've been used to until now. A trip to the corner store to buy some eggs has to be as carefully planned as a bank heist. Know your exits, figure out the angles. Can you trust the people in your gang, or will your spouse turn tail and run when things get ugly after your toddler sees the rack of lollipops?

But if you can do it, if you can make it to the corner store and back with your small child and your marriage intact, the rewards are enormous. Eggs, for one. And secondly, a feeling of accomplishment. You have left the house and returned alive. Congratulations: You are Marco Polo.

Here's what you need to make this dream a reality:

Car Seat

In the good old days, children were tough. They didn't need car seats. They just sat in cars, maybe on people's laps. People would just put babies in the trunk or strap 'em to the roof, crack open a beer, take a big hunk of asbestos and rub it on their face (for luck), and off they'd go.

They just didn't know any better. It's easy to laugh at the naïveté of the previous generation, but remember all that money you lost in the 1990s investing in pets.com? So shut up.

Anyway, now things are different than the free-and-easy baby-flying-through-the-air-because-there's-no-such-thing-as-car-seats 1950s. All children must now be secured to the auto frame by a federally approved child-safety harness system. This system must be installed properly to ensure all mandatory safety standards have been met, and it must match the age, height, weight, blood type, and future sexual orientation of the child.

Additionally, all children must be placed in the rear seat of the automobile, to protect them from the federally inspected air-bag safety system in the front seat which is good for you but bad for them.

That's right. Your kids can't ride up front with you. Not until they're old enough to no longer need a car seat. Under current laws this means they're in the back seat until they're twenty-seven.

This makes things easy because your baby is strapped into a plastic container, facing away from you, in the back seat where you can't reach her. As we all know, babies don't like to be picked up. They like to be isolated away from everybody, ideally turned in a direction where they can't see their parents. Plus, who doesn't like to be strapped into something? So that's another treat for baby.

When driving with your baby in the back seat, try to take it easy. Your baby may be crying, yes, most likely constantly, for the entire trip. But there's nothing you can do about it because you're in the front seat and she's not. She's a back-seat problem. So you're free to relax, tuning out the steadily increasing screaming, devoting your full attention to your driving.

At this point you may notice your knuckles are white and you're going nine times the speed limit so you can get home and get your child out of the car seat before she completes her transformation into the Hulk. This is perfectly normal.

Yes, you probably shouldn't drive that fast, especially while you're looking over your shoulder at the banshee in the back seat.

But on the other hand, at least everybody's strapped in. With all this safety equipment, what the hell, why not have an accident?

Snuglis

Maybe you don't want to drive. Maybe you can walk. Sure, it's fifteen miles. But now that you've crashed your car what choice do you have?

This is where you need the Snugli. The Snugli is a fabric device with a number of straps and buttons and hooks and several warning labels about how it probably shouldn't be used at all by anyone for any purpose.

What is the function of the Snugli? Experts now believe you're supposed to put your baby inside it, somehow, and then fasten some of the straps to your body, probably your upper torso, and then you're supposed to walk around like that.

Thus your baby is right in front of you, where you can deal with her. A side benefit is your baby is on display for all the world to admire. It's like hunters strapping a prize elk to the hood of their car, except the elk usually doesn't puke on the hunters.

A Snugli can be a good choice. Your hands are free, so you're able to do things like wash the dishes, tidy the house, pick up the phone and make a chiropractor's appointment because this kid is eleven pounds now, and so on.

One downside of the Snugli is that, for men, having a baby strapped to your body does not present the most masculine appearance to the world. James Bond, for example, wouldn't have a baby strapped to him (except maybe in that movie where he was played by George Lazenby).

And it's not unknown for the Snuglis themselves to make matters worse by coming in childlike colours and patterns. Even the Lazenby Bond wouldn't wear a Snugli with clowns on it. Not even if it secretly shot rockets.

What can a guy do to counteract this perception? Until they make a leather Snugli, or maybe something in camouflage, there's not much you can do to change the way the world sees you when you stride around with your puking baby strapped to your chest. Our advice to you as a Snugli-wearing man is to change *your* attitude. Don't think of it as a Snugli. Think of it as a baby holster. You know how cops on TV take off their jacket and you can see their shoulder holster? Don't they look cool? Well, the baby holster is *bigger* than a shoulder holster. So it must be cooler, right?

Plus, unlike a gun, a baby is never on safety. It can go off anytime. You're walking on the wild side, Dad. Look out world, here comes a loose cannon!

Stroller

A stroller isn't just a stroller any more. It's part of an entire system, a host of technologies designed to work together to simplify your baby transportation needs.

Most strollers include a car seat, which doubles as a bassinet, baby carrier, and rocker. The stroller itself may or may not contain: shock absorbers, a separate storage unit, a cup holder, a retractable visor, and, probably, wheels.

Most strollers also fold up to fit into a trunk, and can be reconfigured for when your baby turns into a toddler. If you push the right button, many will also transform into a giant attack robot.

From time to time you will come across other parents who have a stroller similar to your own. They may even have the new model, the kind with two cup-holders or the ability to transform into a *better* giant attack robot, one that can tap dance or one that has a heart of gold.

It's natural to feel some jealousy in this situation. But try to get past it. It doesn't matter that their stroller is nicer than yours. What you should be jealous about is the fact that their baby is also better-looking.

Sport Strollers or "Joggers"

How can you get by with one stroller, even if it does turn into nine different things? You need a performance jogger, so you can take your baby jogging.

"But I don't want to take my baby jogging," you say. "Why are you saying I need a jogger? Should I be jogging? Are you saying I look fat?"

Relax, fatso. We know you're not going to go jogging, that much is obvious. But you still need a baby jogger for the same reason you need a high-performance, hi-tech breathable waterproof windbreaker designed for rock climbing, or a titanium sportswatch so durable that it will operate flawlessly on the surface of the sun (where, ironically, it would always be noon).

Why do you need these things? Because they are cool.

And baby joggers are cool. They're constructed from lightweight but durable, space-age polymers designed by NASA scientists. They have quality reinforced grommets, so that if you figure out what a grommet is and you need to use one, you'll have peace of mind knowing it's reinforced. And they have large aggressive tires with big nubs on them so you can really get the traction you need to BMX (baby motocross).

These things say "Hey, look at me. I'm still young. I'm still hip. Yes, maybe me and my baby are currently here at the mall buying bum cream, but later we're going rock climbing! So park your preconceptions at the door, man. This is extreme parenting!"

Of course, everybody knows this is bullshit. But that doesn't matter: they will still love and admire you because, at the end of the day the fact remains that you own a baby jogger, and baby joggers *are* cool.

Paul

Now that you're the parent of a new baby, it's high time you set your financial house in order.

(I know, I know: We keep starting these chapters with phrases like "now that you're a parent." But it's true – we're assuming you *are* a parent – otherwise it's kind of weird that you're reading this book. Also, I suppose it's not really necessary to point out that you're the parent of a *new* baby. If it's an old baby then you're the parent of a teenager or, like, a thirty-year-old. If that's the case, don't worry, it's no longer high time you set your financial house in order.)

Organizing your finances doesn't have to be complicated, like brain surgery. In fact, it's relatively simple, like some sort of basic knee-surgery.

Make a Will

Step number one: make a will. This may seem depressing, even morbid. But it's not. Making a will is both a necessary and simple task. In fact, it can even be fun.

You know those old TV shows, where everybody gets invited to a mansion on an island to hear the will of some rich guy who passed on? They all meet in a big room and watch a video of the dead man reading the will on a screen that pops out from behind a special panel. And at one point the spineless nephew gets upset because the dead guy gave all his money to someone else and the nephew stands up and starts to complain, but the dead guy, on the video, says, "Sit down, Jasper!" Everybody has a good laugh because that is *so* like Jasper to stand up and complain like that, and of course the old man knew it even though the tape was made months ago.

See? It's fun!

Anyway, back to the will thing: get the lawyer to put in there who gets to take care of your kid if you and your partner should both croak (unlikely) or get fed up and fake your own deaths (more likely).

The trouble with picking someone to raise your child in the event of your death is you can't keep the decision a secret, because the whole point of the exercise is you'll be dead (or pretending to be dead) and they won't be able to ask you who it is you picked. So you really ought to ask someone in advance. And choosing *which* relative or loved one would make the best surrogate parent can lead to hurt feelings. Your relatives might feel like you're picking favourites, and there may even be harsh words at family functions. Especially from that weasel, Jasper. Sit *down*, Jasper!

So my best advice is this: when you get fed up and fake your own death, also fake the death of your kid. Life on the lam isn't as much fun with a kid, but it saves hassle now.

Insurance

You should already know this by now, but either or both you and your spouse are supposed to support your child

73

financially. Don't expect this kid to go out and get a job until he's at least six.

That means if you're a breadwinner in your family, you need to insure yourself. Because if you died, and the next day your kid saw some kind of expensive new toy, but couldn't get it because there's no money because you're dead now, he might get upset. And we don't want to ruin your funeral with everybody being sad.

So get insurance. Here's a true fact about insurance: It is now possible to get life insurance that will pay off even if you commit suicide. Easy money! But here's the catch: You can't commit suicide right away. You have to wait five to seven years or the policy won't pay off. So when you're buying insurance, ask yourself, "Can I go five years without committing suicide?" If the answer is no, shop around. You might be able to find a company that makes you wait only four years.

As an alternative, commit suicide really slowly. Maybe you could just take a little bit of poison every day. The advantage of taking several years to commit suicide is you can really work up a really *good* suicide note. It'll really impress your relatives, even Jasper.

Financial experts agree: If you choose the slow suicide option, make sure you do it right – don't mess up your dosage so you die, like, a week before when the policy would have paid off. Now you just look like an idiot.

Educational Plans
It's a good idea to start saving for your child's education. You can't start doing this too early. It's estimated that, by the year

2030, the average drunken college frat party will cost about a million dollars. An all-weekend kegger could cost even more than that. So you need to set aside money *now* to pay for your child's future drunken mistakes.

The best way to do this is through an education plan. You set aside money every year, and when your child is old enough to go to college, she receives the money, with interest. Of course she receives it with interest. Who isn't interested in money? Ha ha! See, talking about education plans is fun.

On the other hand, putting money into an education plan *isn't* fun. Let's face it, saving money is un-fun. Saving money for something that happens years and years in the future is doubly un-fun. But what you're doing is saving money, for something years and years in the future, and *you* won't even get the money that you've saved. You're giving it away! That's got to be the least fun thing you can do with your money. It would be more fun to give it to the dentist, or to get it all in coins and build a big house of coins out by the highway so people could stop and see the crazy coin-house man.

On the other hand, you are getting a reward for your effort. If you *do* save enough for your child to go to college, they might be able to go to college. The operative word here is *go*. Far away. Then you can clear out her room and put something fun in there, like a pinball game.

When you're looking for an education plan, shop around for one that also allows you to save up for a pinball game. A mind is a terrible thing to waste.

Short-Term Money Management

Once you've set up a will, life insurance, and an education plan, it's time to turn to a short-term money management issue that arises from having a baby around your house. And that is this: Once your baby crawls, you can't leave money lying around.

If a baby is crawling around the house and finds, say, a quarter, she'll try to eat it or stick it up her nose or whatever. This is a medical emergency but, just as important, now you're out a quarter.

This is another good reason to pay a lawyer to draft your will, pay an insurance company to insure you, and put money away for your child's education. After doing all this, you won't have a quarter left for your child to choke on.

Scott

One bright September morning, I borrowed twenty bucks from my son. Well, to be honest, I just took the money. He was careless enough to have turned his back, distracted by some overpriced toy or other, and I dipped into the ample stash of loot in his piggy bank. Alas, just as I snatched the bill, he turned his head. His eyes met mine – busted! I made a break for the hallway, navigated the stairs, burst out the front door. Though much younger, the wee fellow could not keep up. Thank heavens for feeble, untested four-month-old limbs!

Later, I began to feel kind of crummy. That is, I did until I glimpsed a story in the newspaper I had purchased with all the money I had left after ordering a latte at Starbucks. It was about a group called Mothers Are Women (a name every bit as controversial as Dogs Are Canines and Landfill Workers Are Odoriferous) and its fight to have breast-feeding recognized as an important food-production industry.

MAW contended that the nursing of an infant represents unpaid work performed by a lactating woman – work that should be accounted for in calculations of the nation's gross domestic product and reflected in tax breaks and extended maternity leaves. A spokeswoman for the group sounded mighty irked about the current lack of recognition of the value of breast-feeding. You got the sense that if she didn't get her way, thousands of women would soon converge on the streets of the nation's capital to burn their nursing bras. "Keeping unpaid work [such as breast-feeding] unaccounted for is a form of slavery," the group declared. "Until we are all free, none of us are free."

Perhaps this is milking a contentious issue, but consider the implications. What if mere recognition is not enough for the breasts? What if they demand more rights? What if they ultimately seek to unionize? What if the ratification vote ends in a one-to-one tie? And what if support sags and the union is nothing more than a bust?

By the time I got home, my fears had abated. I marched right back into my son's room and grabbed the rest of his baptism money. "This," I said, handing it (well, most of it) to my wife, "rightfully belongs to you." I then began itemizing an invoice, if not for the federal government then for my boy, who – it had dawned on me – has been a taker all his life. "You're what's holding this country back," I told him. "Can you say impediment to enhanced productivity?" I waited. He drooled and said something along the lines of "Bweeh." I smiled triumphantly, "I thought not!"

Reading – unpaid work. Playing – more unpaid work. Changing diapers – talk about your unpaid work! If I were attending to the feces of the average guy on the street, I'd charge at least five bucks a go. And let's not forget that in Norway, an apparently progressive country that factors breast-feeding into its GDP, a middle-class father is annually eligible to claim a tax credit for his participation in up to thirty games of Got Your Nose.

And why stop there? Lactating women aren't the only unrecognized engines of our humming economy. I subsequently pledged to form my own lobby group, Mothers and Fathers and Other People Are, Um, People, to press for tax relief related to the fiscal benefits of other natural bodily functions.

Why, come tax time, are we not given recognition for the number of times we've relieved ourselves in a public restroom? The use of such facilities provides an economic boost in the form of more jobs for the makers and cleaners of such essential equipment as the hand blower and the perpetually empty towel dispenser. What about those who perspire in frightfully copious quantities, thus cooling down a body that would otherwise need to be doused with water, our most valuable natural resource?

Given the similarities in our causes, and the fact I've embraced their (wo)manifesto, perhaps the members of MAW would be keen to join my organization – you know, tit for tat.

Eating. For every person on the planet it's a necessity, part of the common human experience that binds us all together. And your infant is no different. For young children, eating is a basic human need, a necessary and enjoyable part of daily life. So of course they don't want to do it.

There are times when your child *will* want to eat, when he will fill his mouth with glee, his little hands enthusiastically reaching out for more. Unfortunately this will never be when there's food around. New medical research indicates that the recommended daily intake of buttons and chalk for children is zero, so you may want to supplement your child's diet with stuff like vegetables and meat or, at the very least, string.

New parents have many questions about food: How can I get my toddler to eat? What's nutritious? How do I get broccoli out of piano keys? What kind of sweater best repels pudding? What's that flying through the air? Duck! ("Duck" isn't actually a question, unless you've recently tried to feed it to your child, in which case you might ask, "I wonder what I just stepped in. Duck?")

Relax. Instead of asking why your kid is throwing food, ask yourself why you *aren't* throwing food. It's a stupid question, but you might as well ask it because asking questions isn't going to help. Duck!

Healthy eating habits begin with the proper equipment: a blender, a mixer, a toaster oven, a mop, a professional dry-cleaning set-up. All these go a long way towards preparing your child healthy, delicious meals that can be easily removed from nearby surfaces.

Perhaps the most important mealtime accessory is the high chair. Most high chairs come with straps, and this is perhaps your first clue about a baby's attitude toward mealtime. People aren't usually strapped into chairs unless they're about to be executed or take part in some high-speed activity. Feeding a toddler is sort of a cross between these two things: they like it about as much as being executed so they throw food at high speed.

You may also want to purchase an infant drinking cup, or "sippy cup." Sippy cups have two special properties: they don't leak, and you can buy about a thousand of them and still not find one when your child wants juice. This is because children hide sippy cups, stockpiling them away for future use much like our friendly mammalian cousin the squirrel.

Although you may blanch at the expense of constantly buying more sippy cups so you'll finally have one of the stupid things around when you need one, rest assured that they will one day make great heirlooms when, years from now, they are found by whoever moves into your house after you.

Many parents buy their children special baby knives and forks. This can be a mistake, as babies commonly shun the fork in favour of eating with their hands, and will only use the knife to defend themselves when you try to strap them into the high chair.

If you do choose to start your infant on a knife and fork, here are the ages children commonly acquire the motor skills appropriate for each item:

8 months	spoon
1 year	fork
13 months	knife
15 months	salad fork
17 months	spatula
18 months	chopsticks, lobster tine
19 months	fondue set
22 months	pruning shears, chainsaw, zester
23 months	George Foreman Grill
24 months	melon baller

For etiquette-conscious parents, the proper place setting for children is as follows. From outside to inside: sippy cup, spoon, knife, *where's the sippy cup?*, fork, napkin, *hey the sippy cup's gone again, why'd we just give him a napkin?*, dessert spoon, *duck!*

Although mealtimes can be difficult, experts agree that your child's reluctance to eat is no cause for alarm. It is just Mother Nature's way of pissing you off. Once you've acquired the proper equipment and techniques, you should be in for smooth sailing: food smoothly sailing across the room in a long graceful arc towards your new sofa.

If you have friends who are parents, you will probably have noticed that when they drop by to visit, there are subtle differences in the things they are now apt to say. For instance, in the time before children, they might have been inclined to remark, "Hey, new coffee table. It's nice." These days, however, they are more likely to declare, "Hey, new coffee table. Get it out of this room before it *kills our baby!*"

See what we mean? *Subtle* differences.

As your child begins to grow and become mobile, you too will begin looking at your home in a new way. Where once you saw a stylish, functional end table, you will now see a diabolical torture device with sharp, laceration-inflicting corners and hard, bruise-inducing surfaces. Where once you saw an innocuous portal from which to draw electricity, you will now see twin hellholes. And where once you saw a chic, expensive sofa, you will now see that while you were reading this chapter your chic, expensive sofa has been smeared in grape juice and goldfish crackers, an occurrence that in itself does not represent a danger to your child unless you happen to remember how much you paid for the sofa.

Parenting manuals typically devote many pages to the taxing process of preparing one's house for a toddler's unsteady gait, curious fingers, and general, all-round resemblance to an inebriated midget. Corporations have amassed huge profits from the manufacturing of devices that prevent young children from being hurt by opening and closing drawers, lifting the toilet seat, or falling down the stairs. Sadly, no corporation has yet created a product that will prevent adults from being hurt while attempting to install these child-safety products.

Still, there's no escaping the fact that a mobile child is a curious child and a defenceless child, and – if you attach one of those Swiffer cloths to his belly – a pretty decent broom. The time has come to take the necessary precautions to render your home a safe environment in which your inquisitive young toddler can explore. Happily, this need not be an arduous, time-consuming chore if you follow our Exclusive Three-Step Plan to a Fully Childproofed Residence:

1. Go to the nearest major airport.

2. Hotwire a truck filled with that thick white foam they place on the runway to slow down and protect crash-landing airliners.

3. Drive home, place the nozzle through an upstairs window and completely fill your house with thick white foam.

We are not going to sugar-coat this: There is a downside to completely filling your house with thick white airport foam. It is, for instance, going to be much more difficult to find your car keys in the morning. Apart from that, and the very real possibility that – given the prevailing state of thick, foamy whiteness – you may wind up having intercourse with the laceration-inflicting end table rather than your spouse (ouch!), it's a guaranteed and risk-free solution to your parental inadequacies. Plus, you can go out for Halloween dressed as a family of lattes.

If you're one of those weird people who object to filling their homes with thick white airport foam, or if another savvy parent has already carjacked the foam-truck from the local airport, there is another way to achieve a childproof residence. Begin by taking a look around your home. Venture into each room and immediately remove the following:

- any furniture with pointed edges;
- any furniture with glass elements;
- any furniture from which a child could fall or jump;
- any furniture.

Next, take a quick inventory of everything that remains in your home – carpets, major appliances, clothes, etc. – and closely examine each item to determine the extent to which it could present a risk to your child. Each item you deem dangerous should be removed. Each item you deem safe should also be removed. After all, the only thing more dangerous to a child than a dangerous item is the one you think is safe. You might be thinking to yourself right now, *Hang on, that doesn't make any sense.* To which we can only reply: Who has more credibility – a pair of esteemed authors who between them have four children and years of hands-on parenting experience, or a new parent who just committed a felony by stealing a foam-truck from the airport?

The important thing to keep in mind here is a legal term known as culpability. Yes, technically speaking, it was your eleven-month-old daughter who, of her own free will, decided to lift the top of the shoebox and examine your prized collection of glass shards, barbed wire, and tainted European cheeses. But in this crazy mixed-up world of ours, it is *you* who will be held culpable. The thinking is that a person of such a young age could not possibly have the mental capacity to gauge on her own the wisdom of stuffing her hand into Daddy's Mystery Box. Note: Adults have attempted to get this whole culpability thing overturned in court, primarily by arguing that the mental capability of a typical grown-up can't be much more developed than that of a child if grown-ups keep casting Rob Schneider in major motion pictures.

Clearly, then, making your home safe for your child can be a big job, but luckily you're not alone. There are a number of gadgets and devices available which, like a faithful robot or a helpful monkey, can assist you in neutralizing the most deadly dangers in that broken-down crack house you call a home.

Safety Latches

Let's be blunt: safety latches are just that, latches designed for safety. Unlike the unpopular and now-illegal "danger latches," safety latches are designed to make cabinets and closets inaccessible to children.

Why? Because your home contains many caustic chemicals and dangerous substances that could seriously damage a child. For example: drain cleaner, rat poison, a DVD or VHS tape of any Kevin Costner movie where he's not a baseball player, and so on. These items need to be locked away from your child, yet kept easily accessible for you (well, except for the Kevin Costner movies).

The good news is that safety latches are quite easy to install, and relatively convenient for an adult to operate. In fact, just about the only real drawback involved with safety latches is that they don't work at all.

Really, do you think a little *latch* is going to keep your kid out of that cabinet? The alluring and forbidden Cabinet of Mystery and Danger? Your child has got nothing better to do but plan and scheme, making multiple "innocent" trips to the kitchen to case the joint. He can make maps and plans and consult with his gang, until one night, when you're not expecting it, he will spring into action and, using a combination of split-second timing and audacity, snatch that drain cleaner before peeling away in his getaway diaper.

A little *latch* isn't going to stop him. Instead, consider hiring a security guard to sit in your kitchen. Yes, it's expensive. But you won't have to buy a bunch of latches so you'll save some money there.

Safety Gates

Safety gates are used to restrict your child's movements to "safe zones" within the house. They are not unlike the Berlin Wall. Your child sits on one side, looking at freedom only feet away. You patrol the wall, foiling numerous plots to get past it. If your child is persistent, she may dig a tunnel.

Eventually, your child will become old enough to travel freely through the house and the safety gate will come down.

Like the fall of the Berlin Wall, this will be cause for much celebration and laughter and – if you're unlucky – a disappointing concert by Roger Waters, formerly of Pink Floyd.

Doorknob Covers

Doorknob covers are plastic metal sheaths that slip over a doorknob. The idea is the child reaches for the doorknob, turns the plastic cover (but not the knob underneath), and then is flummoxed and confused when – gasp! – *the door doesn't open!*

This sets in motion a lifelong fear of doorknobs that culminates in the child working somewhere where the doors open automatically, like a grocery store or an airport, or a futuristic starship.

If, on the other hand, your child *isn't* an idiot, she will see that something fishy is going on with this big plastic cover over the knob and, after a little experimentation, will figure out how to open the door anyway.

You may still wish to purchase doorknob covers. At the very least they will act as doorknob cozies, protecting your doorknob investment from the rigours of air and light which can so often destroy the patina and freshness that we all covet in a doorknob. A fresh doorknob is a happy doorknob!

Anti-Scald Devices

Anti-scald devices are special valves that are installed in your faucets by a certified plumber or, if you don't mind them being installed incorrectly, you. They prevent scalding injuries by regulating the temperature of the water, shutting it off when it gets too hot.

Of course, you *could* just turn down the temperature on your hot-water tank. But turning down the heat isn't a gadget, is it? So unless you're going to turn the temperature down using some sort of special turn-down-the-heat-of-the-hot-water-tank gripper tool, why don't you just shut up, Mr. "Why Don't I Just Turn Down the Temperature of the Hot-Water Tank"?

Also, are you trying to put the anti-scald device industry out of business? What have you got against them? Are you anti-anti-scald device? You might as well be pro-scalding. You sicken us.

Anyway, another anti-scalding option is to buy slip covers that fit over your faucet knobs. You can prevent children from being interested in hot water by labelling the covers "cold" and "boring."

Smoke Detector

Strictly speaking, a smoke detector isn't a childproofing gadget because it also, unfortunately, protects you. But if you don't have a smoke detector already, you should probably get one. Before installing it, take the following precautions:

1. Check to confirm that the wall where you plan to mount the smoke detector is solid enough to hold its weight.

2. Before installing the battery, ensure that your house isn't already on fire. If it is, wait for firefighters to put it out before wasting a perfectly good nine volt.

3. After installing smoke detector, confirm that this is, in fact, your house. If not, leave smoke detector behind and slink out because this is just *too* embarrassing.

Corner and Edge Bumpers

Corner and edge bumpers are small plastic doohickeys that clip onto furniture to prevent toddlers from hurting themselves.

For example, that coffee table may look safe to you, but what if a toddler bumped his head on it? And what's on top of the coffee table? Hot coffee, probably. What if that fell on the toddler after he bumped his head? And what's next to the hot coffee? Most likely a gigantic three-tiered wedding cake. So after the bumping and the hot coffee the child would probably run around in a comical manner and land face-first in the wedding cake. Then he would step on the end of a rake, causing the handle to hit him in the face.

Oh wait. That's not a child. That's Jerry Lewis.

You should probably still get some corner and edge bumpers.

Outlet Covers

Outlet covers are the stars of the childproofing world, the childproofing device everybody thinks of when they think "childproofing device." These little plastic inserts go into unused electrical outlets, preventing kids from sticking fingers in there and getting a zolt or, worse, a zap.

Outlet covers are a good idea, but consider this: when's the last time you had an *unused* electrical outlet? If your place is like our homes, you've got lamps and stereos and TVs and

MP3 players and computers and printers and a lava lamp and a toaster oven and a VCR and a DVD and a camcorder recharging and a crock pot and – to plug all this stuff into – like, three outlets in the whole house.

When it's time to vacuum, there are hard choices. Unplug the lava lamp or the cordless phone? What if someone calls to ask about the lava lamp? Either way, you're screwed. It's enough to make you put off vacuuming for a month.

Maybe your situation isn't as bad, and you've actually got some unused outlets. In that case, by all means, buy some outlet covers. But consider this: if you're going to buy something anyway, wouldn't it be more fun to buy an actual piece of consumer electronics to plug into the wall? In other words, rather than stop up those unused plugs with plastic plugs, why not stop them up with a TV and an MP3 player and a computer and a lava lamp, etc.

Sure, it's an expensive solution. But you've got kids now. They'll support you in your old age.

Other Gadgets
These are the basic tools that should help make your house toddler-friendly. But you must always be vigilant: Your home may have unique hidden dangers not corrected by the gadgets we've covered so far.

For example, say, hidden under the rug in your living room, you have a pit with sharp poisonous spikes. Maybe when you were young and single you thought this was trendy and cool, but now it could be a danger to your child. Consider buying spike foamies, available at any major poisonous spike store.

These clip over the spiky end of the spike, protecting toddlers from the spike and providing peace of mind.

Or, say you own a nuclear reactor. Leaving the core controls where your toddler can reach them could lead to a serious nuclear meltdown. This could be hazardous. In this case you can either purchase a uranium foamy to cover the nuclear material (note: a spike foamy will usually work in a pinch); or send your kid to nuclear-technician school.

That's all there is to it. With just a little common sense, a few minutes of your time, and thousands and thousands of dollars of products, you can make your home a safe one. Then probably it'll get hit by an asteroid, wiping out everyone, but nobody will be able to blame you.

It's weird. We've just had our baby, and yet I still can't see myself as a mother. Is that unusual?

No, it's a typical sentiment among new parents, especially those who are male. Now take off your wife's nursing bra and go help out in the kitchen, fetish boy.

I was surprised to discover that no matter where we go in public, people keep touching our baby. Store clerks do it. Strangers we pass on the street do it. How can I dissuade them from this rude behaviour?

Simple. When you encounter such a person, wait for him to begin to bend down and stretch out his arm. Then whisper, "Careful. It craves human marrow."

Do I need a nanny?

That depends. If you routinely soil yourself and wake up screaming four times a night, then yes. If not, you can try to get by. But you might want to hire one to look after your baby.

We bought a beautiful, vivid mobile and placed it over our baby's crib, but so far he's paid no attention to it whatsoever. Could something be wrong with his eyesight?

Fortunately, that's unlikely. Instead, there's a much simpler explanation: Your baby hates you. Sure, some advice books will tell you that a newborn baby is best able to focus on objects that are between fifteen and thirty-five centimetres from his face, and is therefore likely unable to see the mobile. Scientific poppycock, if you ask us. What's really happening here is that your infant is subtly preparing you for the realization that she'll never, ever like anything you buy for her, even if she pleads and whines for it. Good luck!

Our baby is fat. He's a fat, fat baby. Fat Baby is what we call him. People see him and they say things like, "Whoa, check out that fat baby," or "Wow, that is one fat baby." So I guess what we're asking is: Are you going to finish that sandwich? Because if not, Fat Baby will eat it.

You raise a pertinent and compelling point about the prevailing size differential among . . . um, could you please ask Fat Baby to regurgitate my loafer?

We're probably just being your stereotypical overconcerned parents ;-), but we've suddenly noticed that our four-month-old baby has this weird sort of hair all over his face and body. His nose is often cold to the touch, and he seems obsessed with his own genitals. Oh, plus we've noticed he has four legs now. Anything to be concerned about?

Not to worry: This happens all the time among sleep-deprived parents. Remove the diaper from your dog and ask him to help you find your baby. He's probably tied up out in the backyard.

We heard the doctors and nurses at the hospital refer to an "Apgar test" that they gave our baby. What is that?

Developed by anesthesiologist Virginia Apgar, the test assesses the general condition of an infant at one minute after birth, and again at five minutes after birth. It gauges appearance, pulse, activity, reflex, and breathing. The test is scored out of ten and most babies receive seven or higher, which means they are in good to excellent condition. To put that in perspective, in the moments immediately following birth most fathers would score under three.

I've read that I'm supposed to feed my baby every four hours, but he's such a lump that he often sleeps for six hours at a time and often won't stay awake during feedings. Help!

No problem. There are several techniques you can use to rouse your baby and keep him awake and interested. You can stroke his cheek. You can jostle him, softly at first, and then a little more aggressively. Or you can jiggle your breast. Basically the same things you do to cajole your husband into having sex with you.

Our breast-fed baby is only a couple weeks old, and she's having eight, nine, sometimes twelve bowel movements a day! Is this normal?

Yes. In fact, it's a good sign in newborns. It means the baby is obtaining sufficient nutrients. Doctors refer to it as an "active elimination pattern." Among diaper company executives, it's known by a different term: "Wooooo-hooooooo! We're rich! Rich, I tells ya! *Rich richity rich!!*"

My husband and I instinctively pick up our baby when he starts crying. My mother says we're spoiling the child. Is she right?

Of course she's right! Mothers are always right. And we're not just saying that because your mother is right now, right at this very minute, here in our office, hovering over us as we type this reply. Did we mention the truncheon? No? She has a truncheon. She says she'll clobber us with it if we don't, and we're quoting here, "tell that idiot girl what's what." She says it will hurt. The truncheon, that is. And – *ow!* – you know what? She's right! Mothers are always right.

This may sound a bit odd, but I'm surprised by how, um, explosive my son's bowel movements are. Is it unusual that they're so loud?

Sweet-bearded Jesus, yes! Yes, it is *highly* unusual. You need to get to a hospital right away. Seriously, put down the book, get into the car, and drive to a hospital *now! Why are you still reading this?* For the love of Pete, go. Go right this very minute. Your child's cacophonous fecal detonations place in jeopardy not only his own health but that of (insert ominous orchestral flourish here) mankind itself!

Just kidding. The sounds are totally normal. Or are they?

I can't decide what to do: Should I breast-feed my baby or is the bottle just as good?

There was a time when breast-feeding was resolutely out of fashion, but many years ago now it was acknowledged to be the preferred means by which to provide a baby with nourishment. The thinking of experts is still evolving, however.

Some researchers say a baby should be breast-fed for the first six months. Others say closer to a year. Almost all agree that regardless of duration, the baby should probably be breast-fed by a woman.

Some women are unable to breast-feed, while others choose to feed their babies infant formula instead. If you select this method, it is important that you sterilize bottles and nipples. Then, one day, you will be busy in the kitchen, sterilizing the bottles and nipples, when you notice your child has a crayon up his nose and is stuffing a dog-hair covered slice of processed cheese he found under the couch into his mouth. That is the day you can stop worrying about sterilizing the bottles and nipples.

I'm the father of a colicky four-month-old baby. Last night, in the middle of the night, I had a long conversation with a swollen-eyed, unkempt elderly gentleman who advised me to get into my car, turn the ignition, pull out of the driveway and never ever come back. Should I listen to him?
Swollen-eyed? Unkempt? Seemingly elderly? That was just you talking to yourself in the mirror. As for making a run for it, we doubt you'd get far, what with you having deposited your car keys in the freezer.

I'm going crazy! As soon as I finish feeding my baby, she starts screeching for more food. What am I supposed to do?
You could consider a number of possibilities: You might distract her with a toy, or suggest an alternative activity, or even impose a "time out." Or you might give her more food. Recent

studies indicate that, in moderation, food can be part of a healthy diet.

My spouse and I are totally excited about having a new baby, but we're a teensy bit worried that our lifestyle will be significantly disrupted. Are we right?
It depends. What's your lifestyle like now? Do you leave the house? When you watch TV, is the program usually hosted by a puppet? Does your fridge display many crafts made from glittery painted macaroni? Have you seen more than one Rugrats movie? If the answer is yes, don't worry; your lifestyle won't change at all.

How quickly should I go back to work after having my baby?
Again, it depends. If you just stepped out for a smoke break and suddenly gave birth in the parking lot, you should probably go back to work right now, if only to call an ambulance. On the other hand, maybe this is a good excuse to take the afternoon off. Unless you recently used the "had a baby on my smoke break" excuse.

I just had my baby yesterday and my control-freak mother is already packing her bags and getting ready to fly out here for an extended stay. How can I make it clear to her that I don't want her to come just yet?
Whoa, who's the control freak? You want to "control" whether or not your mother comes to live with you, to be in your house, with bags, when all she wants to do is be around you, constantly with you, telling you what to do and when you're

wrong, which is all the time, and how in her day kids slept and ate on schedule and how your child is going to grow up to be a criminal if you don't wax the kitchen floor? Maybe *you're* the control freak, freak. If you really need to control who comes to your house, when people can enter and exit, maybe you should just go all the way and get a door.

What's the thinking these days with circumcision? My wife and I can't decide. There's a lot of contradictory advice out there.
Whether you choose to circumcise your baby is a matter of personal preference. Many medical authorities say there is no reason to perform the procedure, but some parents may choose to do so anyway for personal or religious reasons. However, all child-rearing experts agree: If you do choose to circumcise your child, you should hire an expert.

This isn't a do-it-yourself project. It can be tempting to get the tools from the garage and spend the afternoon tinkering around with your baby's foreskin, but you really should hire somebody who's done this before. And a *reputable* expert. Not some guy you've met at a bar. You should not hire someone going door to door, offering you a discount because he's got a crew of circumcisers "in the neighbourhood." Many of these so-called freelance circumcisers are con artists, plain and simple. If they start their pitch, you should cut them off short. They would do the same to you.

Our baby has finally arrived, and we still haven't decided whether we want to use cloth diapers or disposables. What should we do?

You should probably decide. After all your baby is here now and it's going to need diapers. And when faced with the decision between cloth and disposable, our advice to you is to make a decision, choosing one of those two options. Also, we're concerned that you said your baby "finally" arrived. Was your baby late? Because, depending on the deal you had with your doctor, if it's more than forty-five minutes late you might get it free.

We put a lot of thought into choosing our baby's name – Jacob – and we're determined that it not be shortened to Jake or Jay. How do we make that clear to our families and friends?

Jacob? That's a stupid name. It's hard to believe you put so much thought into it if you came up with a stupid name like that. We wouldn't worry about people mangling your kid's name. We're sure everybody will get it right. "Here comes Jacob Stupidname," they'll say. "What a stupid name that Jacob has." "Should we call that kid Jake or Jay?" they'll say. "No," will be the answer. "We will use 'Jacob' because that's the stupidest name of all."

Nice work on the name. Your kid will be saddled with it for life, and we're sure she'll always wonder why you chose to call her that.

We just brought home our new baby and our dog is suddenly very jealous. I'm worried about our child's safety. Is there anything we can do?

First of all, by "baby" do you mean "cat," because if so you should let the dog chase it around and get ready for some hilarious cartoon-style tomfoolery! If, however, by "baby" you meant "human infant," the situation is different. Probably the best thing you can do is sit down with your dog and explain to it that this is the last time you will pay attention to it for its entire life.

After all, now that you've got a baby, why do you need a dog? Having a pet is to having a family as de-alcoholized beer is to real beer. It's family lite. In terms of safety, the main thing to remember is never leave your child alone with the dog. Also, never leave several dogs alone together, as they will tend to sit around and play cards, especially if they're bulldogs who smoke cigars and wear little green visors.

We received a jumper at a baby shower, and now our little guy is old enough to try it out. Are they safe?
Playing with a jumper is perfectly safe as long as the baby remembers that negative touches negative and positive touches positive. With that in mind, put it in the trunk and let the kid pull it out whenever somebody needs a boost.

Some of our friends sleep in the same bed as their baby. Others have put up the crib in their bedroom. Are we being bad parents if we place our child in his own room to sleep?
You may want to consider putting an entire crib in your bed. Or you could let the baby sleep in your bed and you and your wife could go sleep in the crib. Or you could see how long all three of you can stay awake. All of these are viable parenting options.

Choose the method that reflects your personal style. Just remember: Whenever you're talking to parents who've chosen a different method, make sure you communicate to them that they are poor parents who have made the wrong choice. In summary, make the choice that's right for you, and be sure to let other parents know they're wrong.

When my baby cries, her chin sometimes quivers. Is that normal?
It is. You might also see an "opening" sort of movement from the "mouth" part of her face, which is where sound comes out. It's normal for your baby's chin to quiver. However if her body then begins to twist, and her toes start a-tappin', and she proceeds to shake her booty, then probably you're looking at that dancing baby animation that was all the rage on the Internet a few years ago. Get away from the computer and try to locate your actual child.

I appreciate the peace and quiet that a pacifier can provide, but I worry that my child will get addicted to it. Do I have good reason to be concerned?
Who cares? The important thing is they should make *The Pacifier* into some kind of movie. *The Terminator* was a good movie. And remember *The Equalizer*? That was good. We think there was also a movie called *The Regulator*, but we never saw it.

Who is the Pacifier? He's a man of mystery, who lives in the shadows and plays by his own rules. But when you need someone to pacify something, he's there for you, along with his sidekick Santos. Also we think he would have a talking motorcycle.

Santos would have a talking motorcycle?
No, dummy, the talking motorcycle ("Professor Wheels") belongs to the Pacifier. Santos sits in the sidecar.

Obviously, we love our baby and don't want anything bad to happen to him. At the same time, we've vowed never to be like the overprotective parents down the street. Are we being irresponsible?
We certainly hope when you went down the street to see these other parents that you didn't bring your baby with you. Down the street is not a safe place for a baby to go. Any number of things could happen to an infant down the street. You could get attacked by muggers, or bees, or crash into another set of irresponsible parents who are going up the street.

So, no, you aren't being irresponsible in vowing not to be like the overprotective parents down the street. Just so long as your child never ventures down the street ever again. In fact, it's best if she spends her whole life inside your house. And by "house," we mean bunker.

Help us out here. Tummy or back? Which should our baby sleep on?
Good luck getting a baby to sleep on your back. The whole time she's going to be going, "Neigh! Neigh! Horsie! Horsie!" And what if you want to get up and watch TV after she falls asleep?

I have a "difficult" baby. She cries when it's too noisy. She cries when it's too cold. She cries when she dirties her diaper, then cries again when we change it. Where can I swap her for a perfect child?

What an absurd query! This is your child we're talking about! You can't just swap her for a so-called perfect child. Although you could try exchanging her at Baby Gap for store credit.

No matter what time we put her to bed, our baby awakens almost every day at five a.m. It's maddening. Is there anything we can do?

There are several techniques that parents can use to ensure they are permitted to sleep until a reasonable hour. Sadly, all of them involve checking into a hotel and leaving your baby in the care of a friend, family member, trained child-care worker, or, in a pinch, anonymous passerby.

THE SECOND YEAR

Your baby is a year old now. You're not a new parent any more. In fact, there's a good chance you've settled into a nice routine that involves sleeping in as late as you want and doing all the fun stuff you used to do. Yay, you have your life back! And you know what that means, right?

It means you're divorced.

Sadly, one of the most common side effects of becoming a parent is that you grow somewhat distant from your spouse. There's nothing sinister about this. It's just the way things work. It's just the logical outcome of the presence in your home of another person – a demanding, high maintenance person whom you must feed and constantly cater to. And even after your mother-in-law leaves, there's still the baby.

Think about it: there are only so many hours in the day. You've acquired a lot of knowledge about babies during the past year, so you probably can't remember how many hours there actually are in a day, or forget to do routine household chores, like taking out the garbage or, say, putting on your pants. Some parents also find they suddenly can't remember certain phone numbers, like their own or 9-1- . . . 2?

So yes, there may be times when you long to once again have that same, intimate relationship with your spouse. There may even be times when you look across the dinner table and think to yourself, "Who *is* that person?" This is especially likely to happen on days on which you are so exhausted that you accidentally walk into the wrong house after work.

Top relationship experts say it's important to work to ensure the everlasting union with your spouse remains based on the love and respect of one human being for another human being, and not the love and respect of one human being for another human being simply because he finally emptied the Diaper Genie.

Parents of a certain age will remember *The Newlywed Game*. It was a game show on which newly married couples would appear in an attempt to win exciting prizes and let an international TV audience know the precise coordinates of where last they had sexual intercourse. The unspoken truth of *The Newlywed Game*? It was a pretty easy game. The contestants had only recently been married. Most didn't have children. They spent nearly all of their time together and were completely focused on each other, which greatly increased the chances they'd match answers to any queries about what their spouse puts on her hot dog.

Our Not-So-Newlywed Game boasts a much higher degree of difficulty. It's a quiz designed to gauge how much you and your spouse still know about each other, and whether you remain as intimate as ever with your loved one or should, on the occasion of your next encounter, politely ask to see some ID.

(Just one note: We use the term "spouse" throughout the quiz. We mean for the word to cover all its potential synonyms, including husband, wife, partner, life partner, significant other, ball 'n' chain, what's-his-nose, hey you, and the biggest mistake of my life.)

1. When was the last time you and your partner made love?
   a) last week
   b) last month
   c) last baby
   d) . . . um, making love? That's sex, right? (Sorry, it's been a while.)

2. What colour are your partner's eyes?
   a) bluish red
   b) greenish red
   c) brownish red
   d) closed

3. What did you give your spouse for your most recent anniversary?
   a) A nice card
   b) A small gift
   c) Seven minutes of half-hearted groping

4. If you walked into a multiplex in which the following films were playing, which would your spouse go to see first?
   a) *The Godfather*
   b) *Caddyshack*
   c) *Caddyshack II*
   d) *Gigli*

(Note: If your spouse answered (a), it means he or she is an aficionado of quality cinema. If your spouse answered (d), it means he or she is Ben Affleck or Jennifer Lopez.)

5. What would your spouse say is most romantic?
   a) A picnic at the beach as the sun sets over the ocean
   b) A homemade dinner served by candlelight
   c) For once in your life not pretending you're still asleep after the kid starts crying at three a.m., you lazy oaf.

6. If your spouse were able to change one thing about herself or himself, what would it be?
   a) looks
   b) career
   c) choice of spouse

7. What is the most exotic place you've had sex during the past year?
   a) bed
   b) the other bed
   c) ... did we say "bed"?

8. What word best describes your spouse's personality?
   a) spontaneous
   b) predictable
   c) perpetually catatonic

9. What were you doing the last time you were up past midnight together?

a) Attending fun dinner party

b) Taking in great live music

c) Engaging in simultaneous sleepwalking

10a. Which song title best describes your first date?

a) "Hot in Herre"

b) "Let's Get Physical"

c) "Who Let the Dogs Out?"

10b. Which song title best describes your most recent "date"?

a) "Could We Please Talk About Something Other Than Our Child?"

b) "Um . . ."

c) "Awkward Silence"

THE GROWTH OF A TODDLER

At some point your child will take her first steps. At first, she will be awkward – timid and tentative as a newborn foal. Except a newborn foal starts walking when it's, well, newborn. Whereas your little slow learner is already twelve to eighteen months old. Ha ha, your kid's dumber than a *foal*!

On the other hand, odds are your kid will eventually learn to ride a bicycle, something most foals never learn to do. Unless they're in the foal circus. But we believe they've shut most of those down. The score is even. Your move, foal.

Anyhow, a child's first steps mark the moment when she has crossed from being a baby into being a toddler. She has reached what child psychologists call a *milestone*. (The word "milestone" is actually a historical term derived from when they maybe had some stones every mile along a road or a path or something, probably.)

What can you look forward to, now that your child is a toddler? She has turned a corner, and where is she going next? Now is not the time to ponder, because she turned a corner and is going somewhere . . . probably right into the coffee table. Go get her!

Walking is just the first milestone of toddlerhood. You have many developmental changes and challenges to look forward to in the coming months.

Tantrums

Up to this point, your baby might have cried when she was lonely or hungry. She may have whimpered if she was cold or wanted to be burped. If her partner was killed two days before retirement in an action-packed gunfight, she may have held his still-warm body in her arms and cried out for revenge on the criminal scumbag who everybody knows did it but whom the law can't touch. *Damn you Brannigannnnnn!*

However, now things are different. Your child will still cry if she's lonely or hungry or if she's stuck in a 1980s-style cop movie. But you also get extra, bonus crying. As a toddler, your child may feel she has the prerogative – no, the *responsibility* – to kick up a fuss if, for example:

1. You attempt to put on her shoes. ("No shoes!")

2. You *don't* attempt to put on her shoes. ("Want shoes! *Shoes!*")

3. The wrong person attempts to put on her shoes. ("Not Mommy shoes! *Daddy shoes!*")

4. You attempt to put on your own shoes. ("Not you shoes . . . me shoes! *Me shoes!* O wicked spiteful fate, why must you turn all my dreams to dust?")*

In other words, your child has now reached a stage child psychologists call "insanity." But relax. This is all part of Nature's plan. You see, Nature makes children become wilful and easily irritated at the same time as it makes them able to walk around your house smashing things. Why both at once? Because Nature is a bastard.

---

* That last bit is implicit.

This is why it's important that we continue to get revenge on Nature by destroying the ozone layer. Take *that*!

Saying No

Part and parcel with tantrums is your toddler's new-found ability to say no. Not no as in "I don't want any more juice please" but no as in "Your suggestion that I drink juice fills me with revulsion and loathing. I am both disappointed and saddened at this unreasonable request, and in the spirit of protest I will now throw a bowl of cereal in your lap. This act of violence is regrettable, but as the juice suggester it is you who bear full responsibility."

Why do toddlers seem to take such delight in saying no? Simply speaking, because they are testing their new-found independence. Until this point your child has been totally dependent on you, but now he wants to "test the limits" and see how far he can go on his own.

So, rather than "annoying" or "bratty" or as a "maniacal hellion," think of your child as being an emotional test pilot. Like a test pilot he is "pushing the envelope" to see if he has "the right stuff," and he's not afraid to "soar like an eagle" even if it means "driving you crazy."

On the other hand, unlike a test pilot, if your little Chuck Yeager pushes things too far, *you're* the one who blows up.

Whining

Children rely on their parents for just about everything: food, lodging, emotional attention, stock-market advice. To get these things they have to get a parent's attention, and that can be difficult. Maybe you're busy watching TV, or cooking a meal, or still getting that cereal out of your lap.

If you are busy, your toddler may resort to whining. She will repeat the same request over and over again, pitching her voice higher and higher, until it can be heard by only dogs and Superman. She is hoping someone will come to her aid – probably Superman because dogs can't speak English and anyway Superman's helpful like that.

Toddlers aren't *trying* to be annoying when they whine. They are just naturally being annoying, as only they can be. But whining creates a dilemma for parents, because ignoring whining means ignoring a child's legitimate needs, while paying attention to whining means rewarding annoying behaviour. What's a parent to do?

There are several schools of thought. One is to patiently and calmly explain to your child that although you have heard and will respond to her request, whining isn't the way to communicate. If she seems to ignore this advice, repeat it, pitching your voice higher and higher until Superman shows up. Then run away and stick him with babysitting duties.

Another option is to derail your child's whining behaviour by acknowledging his need for attention. When he starts to whine, bend down to his level, make eye contact, and really listen to his request. Often, your child will speak more reasonably once he sees you're paying attention. If not, by making eye contact you've distracted your toddler long enough for your spouse to sneak behind him with a net.

A third method is to be nonchalant when your child whines. The theory here is if she sees that whining doesn't "push your buttons" she will abandon it as a strategy. If you can't hide the signs that your toddler's whining is making you tense, attribute your tension to another cause. Say you're worried about the economy, or the environment. Or say you're nervous because there's a bank robber hiding in the closet and if we're not all very quiet he's going to *kill us all, starting with the smallest.*

Lying

Until children are around five years old, they can't really differentiate between fantasy and reality. So many of a toddler's so-called lies are actually fantasies – harmless fibs that are merely a sign of an active and healthy imagination.

Actually, we don't know if that's true or not. We just made that up. But this so-called lie is actually just a harmless fantasy. Take it as a sign that we have a healthy imagination.

Why do toddlers begin to lie? One theory is that toddlers lie because they can talk, and everybody who talks lies. The hilarious thing is that toddlers are just *really bad at it*. For example, you might notice your daughter spilling juice on the floor.

"Don't spill juice on the floor," you might say, not unreasonably.

"I'm not," says your daughter.

Well, come on. You can *see* she's spilling juice on the floor. She *knows* you can see her spilling juice on the floor. The juice is right there on the floor and it's obviously her juice. Your toddler's lie is hardly worth calling a lie, it's so inept. A much better lie would be:

"I have no recollection of spilling juice on the floor or any sort of juice-spilling event. While the material on the floor in front of me may be juice, pending expert investigation I do not accept that said material is in fact juice or, in the case that it is juice, that it is my juice. Furthermore, I do not admit to having juice, handling any juice products, or authorizing any agents to handle juice or juice-related products on my behalf. In conclusion, I repeat that I cannot recall any event that could have led to this unfortunate and tragic juice spill, if in fact there is a spill, and juice is the material that has been spilled."

Now *that's* a lie. If your toddler is lying like that, then enroll her in law school now because you've got a prodigy.

The Positive Side of Toddlerhood

So far we've concentrated on the problems involved in your child's foray into toddlerhood. You may be asking yourself, are there no positive changes that take place?

Of course there are. Let's touch on the positive aspects of toddlerhood in this section:

1. Sometimes they say cute things.

2. They can walk now so you don't have to carry them everywhere.

That's about it. But number two is pretty good, because, man, at eighteen months old those kids are starting to get *heavy*.

Paul

Sooner or later you're going to start reading to your child, and when you do you'll become reacquainted with the world of children's literature.

Kids' lit has changed since we were kids. In the first place, there are a lot more books with holes in them. Holes where you stick your finger through and now your finger is Larry the Lonely Worm or the trunk of James the Elephant or, I don't know, the sandworm in the kiddy adaptation of *Dune*.

I don't think they'd invented the book-with-a-hole-in-it concept when I was a kid. It's a winner! Kids love it! I think it should spill over to adult books. If you like, cut out a hole here and stick your finger through.

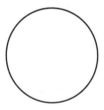

Larry the Worm was very lonely.

There, doesn't your finger bring that sentence to life? Well done. The bad news is we didn't leave a space on the other side of the page so now you've wrecked the book. Way to go, Larry.

I like the beeping, glowing, buzzing gimmick books of today, but I must admit I have a soft spot in my heart for the books I read when I was a child. Kids' books in the seventies were a lot less politically correct than today's stuff. Back then, characters played with toy guns and rode on bikes without helmets and, I think, Curious George smoked.

Read a lot of kids' books and you'll start to see some common themes. I don't know if these children's authors all hobnob at the same literary parties, or if it's just in the air or what, but a lot of kids' writers these days seem to be writing about the important theme of *go to sleep*.

About half of all kids' books end this way. No matter how it starts, by the end of the story Larry the Worm is feeling pretty tired, and he curls up in his cozy wormhole to drift off to sleepy worm land (put your finger in a reclined position on that page), and the book sort of insinuates that, like the worm, the human animal also needs daily rest so maybe you, the child reader, should also consider that it might be a nice time to *go to sleep*.

This never works.

I'm sure kids think it's great that Larry is catching some zees, but it doesn't make them any more likely to lie meekly in their bed and drift off without first demanding sixty glasses of water and making you sing "Baby Beluga" about a hundred times.

Still, it's a nice idea, and I think it should be expanded on. Why not incorporate other positive messages? For example: "After his great adventure, Larry the Worm went back to his nice cozy wormhole, where he *did whatever his parents told him.*"

They wouldn't even have to print that last sentence. The publishers could just leave a blank and you could fill it in with whatever it is you're trying to get your kid to do. Actually, the hell with it, kids can't read. Just leave it out and tell the kid Larry the Worm brushed his teeth or cleaned up his room or *put down the stupid playdough!*

There's not a lot to a children's story. I'm not denigrating the genre, but there are just not a lot of words there. That's why I'm always amazed when there are two or more authors listed on the cover. How many people does it take to write: "See the puppy. Happy puppy. Puppy runs. *Go to sleep.*"

From my point of view, that's easy money. I don't know if the writer and the illustrator split the money fifty-fifty or what, but man, if they do, that illustrator's getting ripped off. The writer spends five minutes writing thirty words about a dog, passes them along, and then the illustrator has to spend six months drawing all these dog pictures, plus, probably, cut the holes in every page so you can stick your finger through. Not fair.

The guy who's really getting ripped off is the guy who draws those *Where's Waldo?* books. He has to draw, like, eight-hundred people standing on a beach. That's page one. I don't think there are even words in those books. That writer's got a good gig: "Where's Waldo this time? Let's see . . . uh . . . at the beach. (*Typing:*) *Where's Waldo at the Beach.*" Hit print and hand it to the illustrator. Call me when the cheque comes!

The other guy who's getting ripped off is the guy who writes the blurbs for the backs of kids' book jackets. "Larry the Worm returns in another one of the educational adventures that have made him a beloved children's favourite for over twenty years. Winner of the prestigious Golden Merit Award for . . ." Stop right there. Your blurb's already longer than the entire book.

That's why there's no *Reader's Digest* for kids. How do you summarize something that's only thirty words long? Unless you just want to cut to the chase, in which case just about every children's book ever written could be shortened to one sentence:

Go to sleep.

Nature is complex. And awe-inspiring. And, depending on where you live, sometimes very snowy. Our point is this: Nature is complex, awe-inspiring, and sometimes, very snowy.

It is only human that, as a new parent, you feel the urge to communicate with your child.* Unfortunately, there is no escaping the fact that, for at least the first eighteen months of your child's life, it is going to be a pretty one-sided conversation: You'll do the talking; your baby will stare ahead vacantly, drool, and, on occasion, reply in unintelligible monosyllabic grunts. In other words, it will be a lot like communicating with most retail sales clerks.

Some parents have difficulty determining how they should talk to their baby. They feel self-conscious. They are uncomfortable using baby speak, that singsong style of cheery, infantile chatter (*Who's a cute wittle baby-waby? Who's a cutie-patootie-rootie?*). At the same time, they feel weird speaking to a young child as though he were an adult ("Replace the toner in the copier, Johnson!") If you happen to fall into this category, there's no reason to worry. That's because there's another communication option available to the self-conscious

---

* The urge dissipates when child reaches age thirteen and/or becomes pierced in three or more body parts.

parent – semaphore, the language of flags. A red flag with three yellow stripes waved four times in an ascending arc means: *Who's a cute wittle baby-waby? Who's a cutie-patootie-rootie?*

The precise time at which a child will begin communicating with actual words rather than *gaaaas*, exaggerated gestures, and hurled cutlery varies greatly. Some children, for instance, will continue to communicate with hurled cutlery well into their sixties. We call these people "circus folk" or, alternatively, "the criminally insane." What's important to remember is that there's only one aspect of the onset of speech that can be stated with any confidence: When your child finally starts speaking, you will have absolutely no idea what she is trying to say.

We are not exaggerating. Is it, for instance, not unusual for a child's first word to be: "Maa." By this, the child means "Mom." Or maybe "milk." Or "moo." Or quite possibly "Watch out! A piano falling from the seventy-eighth floor of a sky-scraper is about to land on your head." As a parent, your natural instinct will be to set out to try to determine what your child is attempting to say. Did she say "moo?" Or was it "Mom?" At which point the piano will land on your head, and the whole "investigating the language mystery" thing will abruptly lose its appeal, mostly because you'll be dead.

Happily, your child's singular speech patterns will become increasingly familiar and as her parents, you will eventually be able to understand the majority of her remarks. In fact, for many months it will be as though you are in possession of a Rosetta stone that enables you alone to decipher the comments uttered by your child. She will say something along the lines of: "Wah ne pay da jin you sake nigh." Other adults in the general vicinity will shrug and look on helplessly. But you will casually reply: "No, honey, you can't play with the Ginsu steak knives. Maybe after your nap."

What you may not realize is that these incoherent utterances are actually a blessing, because most infants and toddlers are not only unable to feed themselves but also to perform one of the other acts integral to survival as a human being: namely, to lie. That's probably why Nature, when it wasn't busy inventing snow, made it so that children who are learning to talk can't be easily understood for months or even years. Humanity wouldn't have stood a chance if babies could enunciate. Consider how our history might have differed:

CAVE BABY: "Grandma stink like poo!"
CAVE GRANDMA: *Beats cave baby with oversized spiked bat.*

Instead, the prevalence of garbled language among infants resulted in an environment far more conducive to the survival of the human species:

CAVE BABY: "Gama sink yike poo!"
CAVE MOMMY [subtly editing message]: "That's a good question, sweetie. What *does* Grandma think of haiku?"

So whenever your child says something that you just don't understand, or something that no one but you can decipher, don't get angry or frustrated. Don't fret over it. That blubbering incoherence is responsible for you even existing in the first place! Embrace it. Revel in it. Soon enough she'll be a teenager and telling you, in perfectly enunciated English, how she wishes a piano falling from the seventy-eighth floor of a skyscraper would land on your head.

FUN ACTIVITIES YOU CAN DO WITH A TODDLER, AND WHY THEY'RE NOT FUN

We all know keeping a toddler entertained can be a full-time job. Some days it can be especially difficult. Maybe it's a rainy day, or maybe your child just has a case of the blahs. Whatever the reason, when your toddler is bored, don't despair! It's time to put on your creative thinking-cap, roll up your sleeves, and come up with a fun and educational parent-child activity that can make your toddler's growing brain blossom!

This won't help of course. Your kid won't like the activity, and you'll feel upset and resentful, but look on the bright side – maybe all that sleeve rolling and hat wearing is making *your* brain blossom.

Here are some fun toddler activities, and why they're not fun:

Colouring

This is an old standby, and nothing beats pulling out the deluxe box of crayons with an electric sharpener and over a thousand colours, including some that aren't visible to the human eye, such as infrared.

Kids love crayons. Lay out some colourful construction paper and they have been known to sit quietly and colour for up to fifteen seconds. Then they will colour on the wall. Or the couch. Or whatever you love most (unless you love colourful construction paper).

Relax. A few stray scribbles is no disaster. Crayons are washable and, besides, if they were using the infrared crayon, no one can see it anyway (except for certain types of bees).

Of course, washing crayon off some valuable item like a coffee table requires your attention and, let's face it, if you had attention to spare you wouldn't be trying to make your kid colour. In fact, you can often find yourself in a chicken-and-egg scenario, where you're looking for an artistic craft to amuse the kids while you clean up the evidence of their last artistic craft. This is the sort of endless loop that physicists now believe can lead to a black hole.

The other thing kids like to do with crayons is stick them into their orifices. Crayons are non-toxic, unfortunately, so this won't harm your children. It would be nice if crayons were slightly toxic. Just toxic enough to produce a slight burning sensation or a tingling that would prompt a kid to pull the crayon out of the orifice. But sadly this is not the case.

Sing a Song

Surprisingly, singing a song to a kid works very well. Your child will love to hear you sing, and she will like to sing along, and this is adorable.

Then the song comes to an end. And she'll want to hear it again, right away, exactly the same. And the nice thing about this is, she doesn't want to hear a variety of songs. She wants to hear the *same* song, and she wants *you* to sing it. The same way you did before. And then she will want to hear it again. And again. And, if you leave it up to her, she will make you continue doing this until you die.

The other nice thing about children's songs is that they are all annoying. They are annoying the first time and constant repetition enforced by a miniature tyrant does not improve them.

Why are children's songs annoying? Because children's songs are written by children's entertainers, and children's entertainers are annoying. And why are children's entertainers annoying? We think it's a defence mechanism. Subconsciously they believe if they are annoying enough, the kids won't make them repeat the same songs over and over.

Of course it doesn't work, because nothing will stop a small child from trying to get you to do the same thing over and over again. So the strategy shows bad judgment. But, hey, if kids' performers had good judgment would they be wearing such colourful suspenders?

Make a "Car" or a "Spaceship" out of a Cardboard Box

Making a cardboard box into a car or a spaceship isn't fun, and here's the reason why: Because making a cardboard box into a car or a spaceship isn't fun.

That's not a car. It's a box. It's a crappy cardboard box and you're trying to pass it off as a car. It's even less of a spaceship. I didn't buy it as a car, but as a spaceship? Come on.

If sitting in a box and pretending it was a car was fun, they wouldn't bother making real toy cars, would they? But they do. And if you buy one of these real, not-made-of-a-cardboard-box toy cars, what does it come in? A cardboard box. And is the cardboard box + toy-car package sold as "Two toy cars, one plastic and shipped inside a second toy car made of cardboard"? No it isn't. So don't tell me that's a car. That's a box.

Yes, fine, your kid could use his imagination to make it into a car or a spaceship. But if he could use his imagination then why is he bored in the first place?

If he has a good enough imagination to be entertained by a cardboard box, then you don't have to think of crafts for him to do. Just drop him off at a grocery store loading bay, home of the Indy 500.

Play With Finger Puppets

Finger puppets are a good choice for people who want to do a puppet show but don't want to make the more serious commitment of using their entire hand. There are times you want to devote just two fingers to the puppet show, leaving the other fingers on the hand as a reserve in case an important three-finger job comes up.

Kids will sit and watch you do a puppet show. Maybe it's because they like the puppet, but it's more likely for the same reason you'd watch if somebody started doing a puppet show for you. "What's this guy doing . . . a puppet show? Why's he doing a puppet show? This is really embarrassing. I'd stop watching but I want to see what he's going to do with the other three fingers."

Banging on Pots and Pans With a Spoon

Banging on pots and pans isn't an activity to keep your kid out of trouble on a rainy day. It's the trouble he gets into on a rainy day, the one that motivates you to come up with some other, non-banging, activity.

If, for some reason, you *want* your kid to bang on pots and pans – because, maybe you're deaf, or for some reason you *hate* your pots and pans and want to destroy them but it has to look like an accident – then go ahead, bang away.

Safety note: If you're going to let your child bang on pots and pans, it's better if she doesn't do it while they're actually on the burner.

Play Hide-and-Seek

Hide-and-seek is not an ideal activity, because it requires you to either (a) hide or (b) seek. Either activity is way too hard for a parent who hasn't had a full night of sleep for the last year.

Think of what could go wrong. You could hide. This is your best option, because if the kid can't find you for long enough, you could have a nap. But then the kid will hear the snoring coming from under the sink, and he'll grab you and shout, "Found you!" and you'll wake up suddenly and try to leap to your feet in the confined space under the sink and – bang! – now you're a sinkhead.

The second option is seeking. But, remember, you haven't been sleeping recently. Your brain is toast, even before the sink thing.

Under those circumstances, if you're going to take on a one-year-old in a battle of wits like hide-and-seek, there's a good chance you'll lose. She will hide someplace you can't find her and, worse yet, you'll get confused and think you're looking for your car keys or something.

And you won't be able to find them either. This will lead you to the conclusion that your toddler stole your car, but when you call the police they won't believe you because it's the third time you've called with the same story.

Just because you now have a kid doesn't mean you can't go out from time to time and treat yourself to a nice meal. However it does mean you now have to consider a new set of options.

When choosing a restaurant before becoming a parent, your thought processes may have gone something like this: Where should we eat? Elegant or casual? Ethnic or not? Will we enjoy wine with our meal?

Now, when considering an eating establishment, you need only ask yourself three questions:

1. Will they bring us crayons?
2. Are there robotic singing animals?
3. When do those crayons get here?

You might like to eat out, but your kids will not. She wants to *go* out. She may even want to go out to a restaurant. She may even want to order food. But when she's actually sitting in a restaurant with food in front of her, she absolutely does *not* want to eat it.

The "family-friendly" restaurant anticipates this reluctance, and so they've prepared a bevy of distractions to keep your child occupied long enough for you to finish your food before the kid goes totally berserk and someone has to call the SWAT team.

Pre-eminent among these family dining aids is the amusing placemat. All family restaurants have an amusing placemat. Usually it's got a picture to colour and maybe a connect the dots and a ridiculously easy, "fun" word search like this:

Find the word. (Hint: it's the name of a drink.)

XXXXXXXXXXXX
XXXXMILKXXXXX
XXXXXXXXXXXX

That's just an example. Of course, a real amusing placemat would never just say, "Find the word." It would say, "Charlie Chicken has lost his word. Can you help him find it?" or "Ernie Eggplant has misplaced his letters, help him out!" or – if the placemat writer is feeling honest – "Frankie Falafel commands you to sit in your chair, colour quietly, and shut up."

Every family restaurant, no matter how humble, has its own crappily drawn mascot – Ronny Rabbit or Frankie Falafel or Sam Sushi or Barry the Poorly Drawn Blob Wearing What Might Be a Chef's Hat.

Not a lot of thought goes into these mascots. "What's a type of food we serve here, and what's a first name that begins with the same letter?" Then the mascot comes to life, drawn by some friend of the restaurant owner, maybe a clever nephew or a guy he knew in school who drew really cool pictures of Snoopy in English class. None of these creations are going to take a prominent place in the pantheon of food industry mascots. Ronald McDonald isn't exactly looking over his shoulder.

Which is as it should be, because the sad irony is this: Kids aren't entertained by anthropomorphized food. Not even a little bit. It doesn't matter how much Peter Pancake or Sandra Sandwich or Trevor Taco jumps or leaps around wearing a big smile and holding an oversized fork, exhorting the reader to connect the dots or help him through the maze or connect the types of fruit with the continents which are known for exporting food products based on that fruit. Kids just aren't amused by amusing placemats. That's because amusing placemats aren't amusing.

Sure, you can draw on a placemat with the provided crayons. That's fun. That's fun for, like, fifteen seconds. Then you can draw on the table. That easily kills a minute. Then, as far as your kid is concerned, it's time to go. Maybe to another restaurant, where you can order more food and ignore it.

This is why, if you're lucky, your restaurant will have robotic singing animals. When famous science fiction author Isaac Asimov invented the three laws of robotics in the 1950s, he left out the fourth and most important law: Robotic singing animals are more amusing than placemats.

Usually, a fine eating establishment that has chosen to install a robotic singing animal won't stop there. They will also have arcade games and Whac-a-Mole and maybe even a room full of balls. Sometimes they even serve food. Delicious, delicious food, straight from the microwave to you. More or less the same food you have at home in your freezer, the same food you went out to avoid because you're too tired to cook but you didn't want to have microwave pizza again.

But it's different eating it out. Now you're eating thirty dollars' worth of microwave pizza and a gigantic cybernetic mouse is repeating its half-hour loop for the third time, and the kid is going crazy from the seemingly mandatory pop refills, and somebody threw up in the room full of balls, and you just want the bill but you can't attract the waiter's attention over the robotic singing and the sound of Whac-a-Mole, and, my God, can't we just go home I need to get something to eat, this pizza was cold when we got it, pull that crayon out of your nose, and when will that mouse shut up?!

So you see: Even though you now have a kid, you really can go out once in a while and treat yourself to a nice meal. Bon appétit!

One of the fringe benefits of parenthood is experiencing an encore of some of the joys of your own childhood – Play-Doh, squirt-gun fights, inserting vegetables into your nostrils – without being thought an utter lunatic by friends or passersby. Also, people will assume that any food stain on your clothing was crudely deposited there by your toddler, which frees you to pay less than full attention to the journey of fork from plate to mouth.

Ranking high among the forgotten delights of youth is the opportunity, and now the obligation, to watch the annual surfeit of Christmas television programs – especially Timeless Holiday Classics, the programs that air every December in the name of tradition, nostalgia, and, most important of all, provide a suitable prime-time venue for advertisements that alert children to the fact that Elmo is now available for retail sale dressed as a chicken.

There is no shortage of new "inspiring" holiday programs, most of which feel as though they were "inspired" by a production-company accountant decreeing, "We haven't yet exploited the potential financial windfall of the lucrative seasonal programming marketplace." But, still, it's not hard for parents to find many of the same shows they watched when they were kids – shows that were synonymous early winter evenings in a time when only Santa Claus went "Ho Ho Ho," and not some rapper dissing his previous three girlfriends.

For those of foggy memory, here's a brief reminder of some of the finest of the Timeless Holiday Classics you'll soon be watching again:

The Year Without Santa Claus

Santa Claus as depressed geezer, grouching that no one cares about Christmas any more. Perhaps best known for the bickering between Heat Miser and Cold Miser, each of whom selflessly takes time from his burdensome schedule of influencing global weather patterns to tell us a little something about himself through the magic of song. "I'm Mr. Green Christmas/I'm Mr. Sun/I'm Mr. Heat Blister/I'm Mr. Hundred-and-One!"

Santa Claus Is Comin' to Town

A story that is profoundly of its time, in that it suggests there actually was a juncture in human evolution when television audiences would accept that a strange man in a bright red suit could stroll into town, in the company of a penguin, and cajole young children to climb up on his lap and give him a kiss in exchange for a gift. Any modern version would by the second commercial break have Mr. Kringle's unshaven mug plastered all over an episode of *Sombertown's Most Wanted!*, hosted by a stop-motion John Walsh.

A Charlie Brown Christmas

Let's face it: There is a generation out there whose members consider *Peanuts* to be the greatest waste of newsprint this side of *Family Circus*. In his later years, Charles Schulz produced comic strips that were so not funny that they were funny, in an unfunny sort of way. But this is *Peanuts* at its zenith – wry, insightful, and touching. In other words, it's the only twenty-two minutes in the whole *Peanuts* video pantheon in which you will not feel an intense hankering to punch Linus in the face. Plus, Snoopy's doghouse is somehow way bigger than it looks! Crazy!

The Little Drummer Boy

Perhaps best remembered for its showcase song, "Why Can't the Animals Smile?" A more insidious melody has never been written – at least not for drum, camel, and orphan. No Christmas special is as joyous, nor is there one so dark, and to this day it's astounding that anyone agreed to put money into this holiday yarn in which the child protagonist is, for the bulk of the half hour, a sullen brat. Still, it's a remarkably moving production, and hey, whaddaya know, it's actually about the guy who put the Christ in Christmas – Christ!

Rudolph the Red-Nosed Reindeer

Unusual: a Christmas special that depicts Santa Claus as a grade-A prick. When he's not bellyaching about his elves or backtalking the missus, the alleged Jolly One is cheerfully enunciating his unique brand of bigotry, in which any critter with a glowing honker is doomed to suffer under his icy apartheid (stay in Massachusetts, Kennedys!). This version of the Rudolph tale is so securely entrenched in the atmospheric fruitcake that several of its leading characters (including Rudolph, Hermey, and the Abominable Snow Monster) were recently rendered as finger puppets available for sale at Starbucks. Seeing it again and again enables the viewer to ponder the smaller questions: Exactly what is supposedly wrong with that doll on the Island of Misfit Toys? Would Hermey really have had time to pull all those teeth from the Abominable? And why the hell do so many viewers insist on referring to him as Herbie?

But the real charm of Rudolph – and, indeed, of many of these old-school shows – is its astonishing dearth of sentimentality, an affliction that corrodes so many of the modern-day attempts at forging a Timeless Holiday Classic. Consider the song "We're a Couple of Misfits," which today would probably be performed as a tearful dirge, but in this special is a peppy production number. And consider that the program's climactic moment – in which Rudolph and Hermey are finally accepted as equals by the North Pole establishment – transpires matter-of-factly, in voice-over no less. Today, there would be a twelve-minute scene of Hermey's boss weeping uncontrollably and Cupid softly decreeing, "Rudolph, you complete us."

Dr. Seuss's *How the Grinch Stole Christmas!*
Towering above them all, like its titular grump above Whoville, is *How the Grinch Stole Christmas!*, which captures the improbable creative intersection of Dr. Seuss, Boris

Karloff, and Chuck Jones. A lot of folks watch this picture each year and kind of zone out, chuckling at the appropriate bits and perhaps contemplating its message about commercialism. Nothing wrong with that. But if you decide to inspect it more closely – the writing, the themes, the animation and above all the imagination that's on display here – you'll find one of the century's most transcendent works of art. Also, that little dog is *hee*-larious!

SIGNS YOU MAY HAVE
PICKED A BAD DAYCARE

- Playground slide ends in blood-coated spikes
- Activities include sewing jeans for sale overseas
- Daycare worker won't give his name
- Staff explain children are restrained in straitjackets because it's "Houdini Day"
- Staff miffed when you insist on taking home exactly the same child as you dropped off
- Child returns home with a tattoo
- Activities include a sandbox, a water table, and a bandsaw
- Daycare worker tries to bum smokes from kids
- Children's nap time from noon to one; staff's nap time from noon to five-thirty
- Daycare lost and found contains several crying two-year-olds
- To enter the daycare you must pass yellow "Police Line – Do Not Cross" tape
- Activities including visiting old buildings and ripping out asbestos
- Daycare kids, left to fend for themselves on a desert island, eventually mount pig's head on a stick and revert to a barbaric pseudo-tribal culture
- The mandatory daycare attire is orange jumpsuits
- Daycare pet "cat" turns out to be a big cockroach

- Presence within the facility of any kind of molten lava
- Whenever you come to pick up your kid they keep trying to talk you into also taking some of the other ones
- Instead of screening a video of *The Wizard of Oz*, daycare shows kids *Oz*
- While digging in sandbox your child finds a mummified thumb
- Sign outside the daycare boasts "Now cleared of all charges!"
- Noontime snack includes one complimentary alcoholic beverage
- Daycare worker is Fagin, a nineteenth-century cockney con artist who inducts kids into a life of crime
- So-called Tinkertoys are in fact brightly painted chicken bones
- Daycare is not a secret satanic cult; they're a very upfront, out-in-the-open satanic cult

FAILED CHILDREN'S TV SHOWS

- *Dora, the Girl Who Doesn't Go Exploring*
- *Marilyn Manson's Tree House*
- *Blue's Clues to Real-Life Homicides*
- *The Industrial Park Next to Mr. Roger's Neighbourhood*
- *Scooby Don't*
- *How the Grinch Stole National Secretary's Day*
- *Bob the Builder Who Blathers On and On about Drywalling*
- *Puppet Autopsy*
- *Clifford, the Big Red Cockroach*
- *Stock Tips with Captain Kangaroo*
- *Barney the Realistically Depicted Dinosaur Who Eats Children*
- *Happy Mr. Funtime, the Big Scary Face Who Just Screams at You All the Time*
- *Law & Order: Clown Squad*

MORE QUESTIONS, QUESTIONS

How should I handle temper tantrums?
Of course everybody's got a different strategy. But when *we're* throwing a temper tantrum we just go with whatever feels good. We might stomp our feet, maybe yell a little bit. If we want to break something we try to go for an item that has dramatic impact but isn't too expensive. Clock radios are good for that.

My friend swears by time outs, saying they have instilled a sense of discipline in her children. But they don't seem to work for my son. What should I do? Are there better ways to teach him about the consequences of his actions?
Time outs have been used throughout history. In fact, many scholars now believe that the Roman Empire never fell; it was just behaving so badly it's now having a really long time out. If time outs aren't working for you, you might want to try a new technique called a "time in." Time ins work like this: If your child is misbehaving, he has to spend some time *in* a little cage in the basement.

Now, some people think it's cruel to put a child in a little cage in the basement. But it's not. Kids love the zoo, and the zoo is basically a collection of cages. We're not saying you should put some kind of monkey or snake in the cage with the kid. That's not what we're saying at all. But if the cage thing doesn't work on its own, you might want to consider it.

I'm finding this book really helpful. Have you guys written any other books that I could rush out and buy multiple copies of at full retail price?
How kind of you to ask! Sure, we've written several other books. We had some minor success with an unauthorized biography of Paris Hilton. We've also ghostwritten a few books, including the authorized biography of Paris Hilton.

I'm beginning to suspect you're making up these questions. I mean, that last question was pretty far-fetched. By the way, is there an address to which I can, as a symbol of my appreciation for the efforts you expended in creating this book, send you 35 per cent of my pay cheque each week? Hey, wait! See what I mean? Nobody would actually ask that, would they? You guys deserve the Pulitzer.
You flatter us – though, frankly, not sufficiently for a non-existent person we created to flatter ourselves.

We've decided it's toilet-training time in our house. Is it acceptable to bribe children?
Of course! Being paid to poo is the dream job of any healthy adult. So why not make that dream come true for your child? This leaves the question of price. It's not considered polite to haggle too much before the fact. Let's see what you produce, and we'll settle a price then. If it's more than we need, we

might let it pass, but that doesn't mean we won't buy more later because of course there's plenty more where that came from.

My daughter has started biting other children. What can I do?
Biting other children can be an important warning sign, along with some other indicators. Has your child been avoiding sunlight? Is she afraid of garlic? Do crucifixes burn her? Have you noticed that she turns into a bat at all? If your daughter does turn out to be a vampire, try not to make too big a deal of it. It's actually an advantage around Halloween.

My child seems to constantly bump into things these days – walls, chairs, even people. What's wrong with him?
Relax. He's just learning to walk. There's nothing wrong with your child.*

I'm beginning to get concerned. Every other child in my son's playgroup has started walking, but our boy doesn't show even the slightest interest in trying. Should I be worried?
No, you should not be worried. You should be anxious and panicky. Worried parents get patronized and told to "not worry so much." Anxious, panicky parents get doted over and handed prescriptions for expensive mood-altering drugs.

How do I know when it's time to buy new shoes for my daughter?
This can be trickier than it might seem. Because children tend to outgrow their shoes before they wear them out, parents

---

* Does not apply if your child is in fact you after a dozen Michelobs.

must pay close attention for certain warning signs that a child's shoes are becoming too tight. One reliable warning sign is blood. If, when removing your child's foot from her shoe, you notice the presence of a large quantity of blood, this may be a sign that the shoe is now too small. Another warning sign is an affliction commonly referred to as Freakish Mangling of the Foot – or as doctors call it, Aiiiiieeeee! Maybe a rhyme will help you remember: *If the feet be mangled and bloody/it's time for new shoes, buddy!*

On the one hand, I'm happy that my son is learning how to eat on his own. On the other hand, I'm getting pretty tired of the mess. He gets more on him than in him, and more on the floor than anywhere else. What can I do?
Let me answer your question with a question: Do we bother you with *our* problems? Buy yourself a mop, Sherlock.

Our kid makes constant comic reference to his poo and pee. He thinks it's really funny and seems to want to think and talk about nothing else. What should we do?
Two options come immediately to mind: 1. Attempt to dissuade him by doing your best to not react to any comments about his bodily functions. 2. Get him an agent and a three-series sitcom deal with Fox.

We've been dealing with separation anxiety lately. Our daughter used to be fine with a babysitter, but now she freaks out whenever my wife and I go out for an evening. She grabs hold of my pant leg and won't let go. What can we do?

Take her with you. Where are you guys going anyway? Out for dinner? God, that's going to be tedious – two tired married people staring glumly at their plates and trying to remember when they had conversations that weren't about doo-doo. The kid will be bored off her nut inside of five minutes. Next time you go out, she'll be clinging to the baby-sitter's leg screaming, "Don't let them take me! Me hate uncomfortable silences!"

My friends are subtly, and not so subtly, suggesting to me that now that my son is more than a year old, the time has come to wean him from the breast. But I still like breast-feeding him. Is it wrong for me to continue for a long while yet?

Heavens, no. In fact, you're doing a lot of good by continuing to breast-feed your son. By that, we don't mean you're doing any good for the child, who long ago ceased requiring your breast milk. The good you're doing is really more of a public service. Think of it this way: Every mother needs a friend whose peculiar, hippie-dippie, crackpot style of mothering makes her mothering seem normal and competent by comparison. So thanks! Thanks for continuing to breast-feed your child into his second year! Now do everyone a favour: Also pledge to raise your child as an oboe-playing vegan who never watches TV. Other mothers *love* that one.

Like most parents, we cherish nap time. It's our only chance to get a break. But we've noticed that if our child falls asleep for even a few minutes in the car or stroller, he won't go down for an afternoon sleep. Why is that?

This question has divided researchers for years. Some believe the phenomenon has its roots in a signal generated in the brain, which essentially convinces the body that it has had sufficient rest even if a sleep cycle is interrupted after only a few minutes. Other researchers are skeptical of the science behind this thesis and instead believe that some infants possess a component to their genetic coding that compels them at every opportunity to – in the vernacular of academe – "totally screw over" their parents.

My husband and I have been arguing about the proper way to set limits with our child. I agree that we shouldn't spend our days yelling, "No!" but at the same time I think we're asking for trouble if we don't instill some sense of discipline. I want to punish my daughter every time she disobeys. Am I being cruel or sensible?
Depends how you define "cruel." If you define "cruel" as "nasty, brutish, unnecessarily unkind," then yes, you're being cruel. If you define "cruel" as "helpful, friendly, kindly" then, yes, you didn't graduate from high school.

I'm a stay-at-home mom and the thing I find most exhausting is that my daughter never wants to do anything for more than a few minutes. Her attention span is non-existent. What can I do to encourage her to focus on an activity for an extended period of time?
We know mothers in a similar situation who have had a lot of success with a specific type of child-centred craft. This particular activity uses a lot of string, so you might want to stock up. What you do is sit down with your child and cut off a couple

of big pieces of string. With us so far? Good. Then you take the longest piece of string and you use it to tie the child to the chair. After this, the craft becomes kind of free-form and improvised. Most mothers just watch soaps for a couple of hours or curl up in a ball and weep uncontrollably. Whatever works for you.

My friend has a beautiful, charming daughter but she – my friend, that is – has turned into a complete nutjob. She's overprotective, she's always stressed out; she doesn't seem to realize that her child is such a well-behaved darling. Are there any subtle ways that I convey my belief that she should calm down and just relax a little?
If you're really her friend, you'll find a way. Don't be judgmental – just emphasize that her daughter is a dear and that you yourself have found contentment in being a more relaxed parent.

My friend just subtly conveyed her belief that I should calm down and relax a little as a mother. Can you believe it?
That meddling bitch.

This may sound crazy but my toddler seems to be obsessed with his own feces. Whenever he has a bowel movement, he tries to remove his own diaper so he can examine the contents. First of all, is this normal? And second, what's the most effective way to discourage him from this behaviour?
We wouldn't be concerned. This is a totally normal behaviour and nothing to be worried about – assuming your child

has swallowed some diamonds and is waiting for them to pass.

Is your child involved in a diamond-smuggling ring? It can be hard to tell, but here are some warning signs: Does your child travel to exotic locations all around the world? Does he suddenly own a number of unexplained luxury items such as fast cars, high-end stereo systems, and those expensive Lamaze-brand baby toys? Is the FBI constantly trying to get him to "flip"?

It's normal for children to go through a diamond-smuggling phase, and eventually your child should move on to more mature activities such as extortion or insurance fraud. The best thing you as a parent can do is support your child and set firm guidelines about how much time he can spend down at the businessmen's social club with his new friends.

We've read that baths are the best way to calm a child and signal that it's the end of the day. But our girl has a palpable fear of water. Should we still force her into the bath?
Maybe the fact that you've been "forcing" her into the water might have something to do with her now being afraid of the bath. Did you ever think of that? Open your eyes! It's not too late to transform bath time from a terror-filled carnival or mayhem into a tranquil and relaxing experience that only has a medium amount of terror. Here are some guidelines:

1. When it comes time to gather your child for the bath, don't wear big hooded robes and weird amulets and play eerie chanting music. Also, consider not having big knives and butcher implements attached to hooks all over the bathroom.

2. Stop referring to bath time as "the reaping." (Instead of "The time of the reaping is upon us," say "Time for bathsies, honey!")

3. Instead of having your bath outdoors in a big cauldron filled with carrots and onions, consider having it in a "bathtub." Your home may in fact already have one of these; they're normally located near one of the toilets.

4. Stop going on and on about how the French revolutionary Jean-Paul Marat died in the bath.

5. Yes, it's important to conserve water. But maybe it isn't such a good idea to give your child and your biting piranha fish a bath at the same time.

6. After the bath, read your kid a story, but maybe not one by Stephen King. And if it is by Stephen King, maybe it's not a good idea to insist that the story is real. And if it is by Stephen King, and you insist the story is real, maybe go with *Stand By Me*.

7. Get some bath toys. Like a duck or something.

I'm shy, so naturally I was worried that my son would be similarly reserved. Turns out he's extremely social, to the point that he immediately cottons to strangers as though he's known them since birth. What's the best way to teach him that maybe he ought not to be so trusting of people he doesn't know?

Interesting that you'd look to complete strangers for an answer to this question. But we'll do our best: First of all, has your son just been born in the last few minutes? Because if so, this might explain why he cottons to strangers as if he's known them since birth. He has. If that's not the case, there are a few ways you can discourage this unwanted stranger cottoning.

1. Show your child the 1970s Robert Redford, Paul Newman classic *The Sting*. This will teach him that not all strangers are trustworthy. In fact, some are lovable conmen engaged in an elaborate ruse involving a fake casino designed to get revenge on you because you ordered the death of their mentor.

2. When you take your child out in public, dress him up like a wolverine. Strangers will think twice about approaching this, the most dangerous member of the weasel family, even if he is wearing Baby Gap and clutching a Dora the Explorer doll in his dangerous talons.

3. Show your child the 1990s Anjelica Huston, John Cusack vehicle *The Grifters*. (Actually, this is a little bit like strategy number one, but you get to see Annette Bening naked.)

Wolverines don't have talons, do they?
No, not in real life. But your kid's wolverine suit should have talons because, we think, a wolverine with talons is less approachable than the regular, non-taloned version.

I always laughed at how attached the Peanuts *character Linus was to his blanket. But now I'm not laughing, because my toddler has a fit if ever she's separated from her teddy bear. Is this normal and harmless for a child or does it hint at the fact she may have an obsessive personality?*
We always laughed at *Peanuts* too, but you know what's really funny? *Calvin and Hobbes*. Man, that kid and his stuffed tiger would get themselves into the craziest situations! You know what else we like? *Andy Capp*. That lovable cockney is funny because he drinks too much. We guess we like *Hagar the*

Horrible too, but not as much because I don't think, in terms of historical accuracy, a Viking would have a best friend with a nickname like Lucky Eddie.

I'm going crazy! It seems like just yesterday my little guy was taking his first steps. But now when I put him down he's off like a shot, no matter where we are. I'm afraid I'm going to lose him. Is it acceptable to use one of those toddler leashes?

Absolutely, although child psychologists believe it's demeaning to use the term "toddler leash." Instead, when the child is present, refer to the leash as the "tether of servitude." If you do use a leash for your child, consider wearing Rollerblades and getting your kid to pull you. If you have a large family, you could have an entire pack of toddlers pulling you and whatever heavy cargo you wish to transport. Who knows? After a few months of training you and your "pack" could be ready for the Iditarod, an exciting 1,150-mile-long dogsled race across the frozen Arctic. Children love animals, and sports can give kids a sense of accomplishment.

THE THIRD YEAR

As if adjusting to life with a child is not challenging enough, the new parent must also learn how to handle encounters with other new parents. This is more difficult than you might expect because being a new parent can radically change the very essence of a person's being. Carefree individuals can become big freaking-out stress monkeys. Amiable layabouts can become joyless taskmasters. (Not you, of course. We're not talking about you. Heavens, you haven't changed a bit!) And in very rare circumstances, perfectly ordinary, likeable people can abruptly transform into one of the most sinister parental forms known to humanity, not to mention most parts of the animal kingdom: the Outdoer.

Not familiar with the Outdoer? Consider the following case study:

Most people would acknowledge that Valentine's Day is for sweethearts and for lovers, and possibly for neglected wives who hope the dubiously mandated romance of February 14 might somehow prompt their husbands to initiate a little mercy sex. Logic would dictate – and Logic's secretary would dutifully transcribe and eventually get around to posting the remarks in the office – that this day of corporation-crafted, Hallmarkian sentiment is, all things considered, not an especially important occasion for a two-year-old child.

Sure, it's possible that, were you to ask a two-year-old if he would be your Valentine, the child would reply yes. Then again, odds are pretty good the same child would say yes when asked to speculate whether a full-grown antelope would fit comfortably up his left nostril. He's still a little fuzzy on yes. Let's put it this way: most young kids have trouble enough comprehending the intrinsic relationship between fart and stink. There's really no point trying to explain how the legendary bow-and-arrow prowess of some effete, scantily clad Roman god today means that Daddy has to pay usurious prices for a dozen roses on his way home from work.

Logic would therefore further dictate that two-year-old children should not be expected to show up on February 14 hauling an arsenal of heart-covered cards and love-themed snacks for their daycare chums, many of whom are probably also two years old, and therefore a good ten years away from their first genuine brush with romance (six years for those who happen upon the "special" novels in Mommy's bedside table). Alas, in this case Logic's dictation would be drowned out by the stentorian exclamations of over-anxious, overachieving parents reminding their clueless tykes to dutifully distribute the punched-out, individually labelled *Peanuts* cards and elegantly crafted Cellophane bags of cinnamon hearts.

You know who I'm talking about: the Outdoers. These are the image-conscious parents who make Martha Stewart look like a domestic slacker. The parents whose urge to outdo is sufficiently twisted and perverse to make one regard all of human history with a fresh perspective. Officially, the Catholic Church recognized three St. Valentines, and all of them were martyred. Those familiar with the work of the Outdoers could make the persuasive case that the three were very likely stoned to death by irate parents after sending children to daycare on February 14 without a Tupperware container filled with Rice Krispie squares, um, hearts.

Ancient lore has it that Cupid was a god who could master men's minds, make their bodies go limp, and effortlessly subdue their wills. Now he's consigned to an eternity of servitude at the manicured hands of uptight moms whose motto is Outdo for Fear of Being Outdone. Two-year-olds do not have sweethearts or lovers. *Some of them don't even have teeth.* But this does not dissuade the Outdoers. The Outdoers embrace any excuse to attempt to outdo other parents. Christmas gifts must exceed established price limits. Loot bags must overflow with gadgets and gizmos. Bake sales must be stocked with elaborate pastries instead of rudimentary cupcakes. And children can never, ever be sent empty-handed to daycare on anything even resembling a holiday or occasion. Give the Outdoers a couple more years and our kids will emerge from kindergarten on Arbour Day with robust saplings peeking out from their backpacks.

It is understandable, and also right (oh, and fun!), to loathe the Outdoers, not because they are so annoying (well, not *just* because they're so annoying), but because the urge to Outdo is typically derived not from joy but from fear. If an Outdoer does not outdo, it means they have been outdone. The ritual, the occasion, the event: most likely it means nothing to the child. But dammit all, the Outdoer's going to bring fifteen punched-out Valentines to daycare, and if your kid doesn't do the same then she is going to find you, and she is going to look you in the eye and she is going to smile her "You Lousy Mother" smile.

In the mind of the Outdoer, you're only a good parent if you're seen to be a better parent than all the other parents.

Paul

Okay, bragging time: My daughter Katie knew the entire alphabet well before she turned two. I think that's earlier than normal. I'm not sure; I'd look it up but, well, I don't have time. I've got a two-year-old. Did I mention she knows the alphabet?

It's all about the alphabet at our house. Katie's very alphabet-oriented. It's her favourite topic of conversation, right up there with Elmo and pooping. If Elmo could poop out the letters of the alphabet, I think my daughter would really like that.

She yells out the letters when she sees them. She yells out the letters when she sees the things that go with the letters in her alphabet book. (I for ice cream! X for X-ray! Well, she's never actually seen an X-ray. Or a xylophone. They need to invent more X things, just to make life easier for people who write alphabet books.)

She also sings the alphabet song. Incessantly. I guess that's not a surprise, seeing as kids her age either refuse to do something at all, or insist on doing it over and over again. But I would estimate, conservatively, my daughter sings the alphabet song, oh, ninety billion hundred million times a day. Is that a lot? I'm sure there's been a study. I don't have time to look it up.

Of course, she has no idea what the letters of the alphabet actually mean, or that they in fact mean anything. As far as she's concerned they're just (a) the lyrics to her favourite song, (b) a sort of scavenger hunt, where people of the world have banded together and placed written letters all over things just so when she walks past she can call them out.

I think it's going to be a bit of a letdown when my daughter discovers that the whole of written language isn't a giant agreement between all of the world's people for the last few thousand years to create visual illustrations of the lyrics to her favourite song. That letters are there for a purpose – unless they're magnetic and stuck to the fridge.

The alphabet obsession has snuck into our lives too. Like countless parents before us, we use the alphabet as a code to talk over our daughter's head. "Hey, should we buy some C-A-N-D-Y?"

This has mixed success. Two downsides: first, spelling out the letters I-C-E C-R-E-A-M takes a long time, so you're tempted to just say "I-C-E cream." But this sounds like "icey cream," which still sounds pretty good. In fact, if they actually invent a something called "icey cream," let me know. I'll be in line for that stuff – I bet it's actually *better* than ice cream.

So we've given up on the alphabet code for ice cream, which is unfortunate because ice cream-related communication is still very sensitive and must be carried out in secret. We have yet to come up with a suitable substitute – pig Latin's out because, what's "ice cream" in pig Latin? E cream ic-ay? Ic-ay eam-cray? E-ic-ay cream I-ay? I don't know the proper usage.

We're thinking about using carrier pigeons.

The second hazard of the alphabet code is that it's addictive. The other day, after eating some P-I-Z-Z-A, I asked my wife to pass me the B-I-L-L. This probably wasn't necessary because, as far as I remember, my two-year-old hasn't once yet offered to pay for a meal. How cheap is that? (Plus, I suspect my wife actually buys all the Father's Day gifts.)

In spite of its flaws, spelling out words is a time-tested method of childproof communication. It makes me wonder how parents kept secrets before the invention of the alphabet. Were Ancient Egyptian parents always saying things like, "Hey, you want to stop on the way home for a nice bowl of ankh symbol-ferret-profile of a guy wearing a big hat-large scary eye?"

And what do parents in China do? "Let's stop for a sort of a box-like squiggle with two brush marks above it and a diagonal line going through." Maybe Chinese kids get to eat all the ice cream they want.

Who knows, maybe that was the original purpose of the alphabet. They invented it just so people could keep secrets from their kids. Or maybe it was just to provide lyrics for the alphabet song. Or to make Scrabble more practical.

I don't know. Like I said, I'd look it up but I don't have time. I have a two-year-old.

Scott

When you have two children in diapers, and a large dog, and a functioning intestinal tract of your own, it is quite natural to arrive at the conclusion that your life is governed by excrement. Catching a whiff of it, picking it up, wiping it away, disposing of it. It's the circle of strife.

I'll admit it: I have never been nuts about spending time in close proximity to feces. Call it a quirk. So when my first son, James, was born, I resolved to promptly master the diaper change in the hopes that I might – as the months, and the solid waste, would pass – refine the ordeal into an endurable ten-second process. I thought of it in terms of a pit stop: Get in and out as fast as possible. All nice and Zen-like. Diaper off, diaper on. Just like *The Karate Kid*, but without the ludicrous romantic subplot.

Alas, the thing about a child's poop – and really, in the end you can only refer to it as poop, or poo, because calling it anything else makes you sound like a militant nutbar or, worse, a fetishist – is that it . . . well, let's just say that it evolves. There comes a time when even the fastest of hands can no longer rival its swift, devastatingly odoriferous efficiency. Thoughts turn to toilet training, if only because teaching a child to use the facilities seems easier and more cost-effective than installing a tiny pine-tree air freshener in each nostril.

For their part, the experts insist that "toilet training" is a misnomer. Some even call it "toilet learning," a reflection of the fact that the youngster in question can't simply be tutored like a disobedient pooch. Others suggest employing the more humble expression "toilet using." In the end, my wife and I settled on a name that seemed a more apt description. I called it "Arrrgh!"

Consider this sequence, which for several months played out during the supper hour at our home: James gets up from his chair and wanders off. Astute parent: "Do you need to poo?" James shakes his head, which subsequently adopts a distinctly reddish hue; he emits a faint grunt and his eyes bulge. Either he's relieving his bowels or he's auditioning for the role of Exploding Head No. 3 in another sequel to *Scanners*. The astute parent rises: "James, are you pooing right now?" A lightning sprint to the bathroom is recommended. "No, I'm not pooing!" He stands in place for a minute more. A toxic waft crosses the room and settles ominously over the dinner table. "Daddy," James says, and not unhappily, "I pooed."

Arrrgh!

The authors of those parental advice books tell you to wait, to be patient, not to badger the child in matters of elimination, all of which leads you to believe that these authors are patient, understanding people who have never actually had children – or at least not any who exhibited a tendency to defecate.

When James turned three, we decided it was time. To our chagrin and frustration, he decided it wasn't.

We talked about it. We discussed the fact that big boys don't wear diapers. We talked about the ease of using the toilet. No dice. We bought a small plastic potty. Nothing. Purchased the absurdly pricey *Blue's Clues* toilet ring. No takers. Bought several inspirational books in which the plucky protagonist endures several "accidents" but ultimately triumphs in the whole pee-pee business, much to the rapturous delight of all. Liked the stories, didn't exactly get its moral. To take advantage of his fondness for superheroes, we purchased briefs that depicted Spider-Man, Batman, and Superman engaged in valorous pursuits. James loved the underwear. He loved the underwear so much that he rushed to put on a pair. Right over top of his diaper.

Sigh.

We worried. We fretted. We pictured James posing for his prom-night photos, a beautiful young woman on his arm, a Huggies Pull-Up slightly puffing out the crotch of his stylish trousers. We concluded that our supportive, Up-With-People chatter was getting us nowhere besides the diaper aisle of the local supermarket. It was time to adopt more creative and proven methods of persuasion.

We promised him candy. We promised him toys. We promised him bigger, better toys. Grandmothers got in on the bargaining. My mother – ever keen to see James master this particular skill, since back in her day everyone was apparently toilet-savvy by the age of roughly four minutes – promised him a toy that retailed for seventy dollars. Finally, we had his attention. James really wanted that truck. He talked about the truck a lot. Unfortunately, he mostly talked about the truck just after soiling a diaper.

Deep sigh.

At this point, it occurred to me that the stability of the national economy rested with my eldest son's rectum: If only he would deign to use the toilet, a formidable reserve of disposable income would be injected into the retail sector, fuelling job growth and economic prosperity across the land.

So, to recap: At this point, we were employing a brilliant, three-pronged approach involving bribery, extortion, and (I'll leave out the details of this part) shameful, barefaced pleading. Alas, as strategies go, this one made the guy who dreamed up New Coke look like friggin' Einstein. James was going through diapers like a chain-smoker through Marlboros. I can remember one spring day when he needed to be changed nine times. Nine times!

There's a Raffi song called the "Numbers Rhumba." At one point Raffi sings, "Number two all day long!" Raffi didn't mean it in the scatological sense, but the song nevertheless became the soundtrack of our lives. Number two was dominating our waking hours. As I changed James for the ninth time that day, I caught a glimpse of Mickey Mouse, whose cheery image decorates the front of each and every Huggies Pull-Up. I swear he was smirking.

Four months and a pile of soiled Pull-Ups the size of a small European principality later, on the final day of July, while we were away at a cottage – away from the *Blue's Clues* seat and the toilets-sure-are-great! books – we at long last witnessed the triumph of our persistent nagging. James was, almost to the day, three-and-a-half years old. There was much rejoicing. The next day, we went to a toy store in Parry Sound where James selected as the first instalment of his reward a bug-collecting kit and a portable Snakes and Ladders game. He announced to several people in the store that he had pooed on the toilet. For some reason, they did not seem nearly as jazzed about it as we did.

Meantime, my mother, ever ruthless in the ways of negotiation, slyly attached a condition to her bribe: only seven successful trips to the can would secure the mighty truck. A week later, while we were driving home from daycare, James phoned his Grandma, and began the conversation by shouting, "It's time to get me that truck!" From the front seat, I could hear Grandma's tinny cheers through the cellphone earpiece.

At that very moment, across the car, plunked in the other child seat, our one-year-old son, William, emitted a faint grunt. His face adopted a distinctly reddish hue, and his eyes bulged.

CARTOON VIOLENCE

There are, we're told, risks in permitting your young child to watch television. Some researchers contend that even limited exposure to scenes of cartoon violence will prompt youngsters to grow up to be more violent than other adults. But is that true? As a grown-up yourself, and one who was probably exposed to cartoon violence as a child, take the following quiz to find out.

1. When I become upset with a friend or co-worker, I
   a) confront him to initiate a frank and honest discussion.
   b) drop an anvil on his head.
   c) drop an anvil on his head using a complex series of gears and pulleys, and then, when it doesn't work, I go and stand directly under the anvil and poke it with a stick.

2. When I see a sign that reads "Danger, falling rocks," I
   a) ignore it.
   b) drive more cautiously.
   c) instinctively reach for my little black umbrella and a small wooden sign that says, "Help!"

3. When I receive a birthday cake, I
   a) smile appreciatively.

b) mourn for my lost youth and ponder mortality.

c) improbably fail to notice that the candles are, quite obviously, made of dynamite.

4. If I owned both a cat and a bird, and the cat was constantly trying to eat the bird, I would

a) keep them in separate rooms.

b) give away either the bird or the cat.

c) not worry about it too much because I'd know that if the cat ate the bird I could always say, "Bad cat, bad cat!" and slap the cat on the backside, causing the bird to pop out of its mouth, intact and unharmed.

d) also get a boxing kangaroo.

5. When, during the course of my daily activities, I attempt to operate a catapult

a) the large rock falls on me.

b) I hide where the large rock won't fall on me, but then the entire catapult flips over and falls on me.

c) I hide where neither the large rock nor the catapult can fall on me, but then the catapult does nothing, prompting me to get up onto the catapult to see what's wrong, at which point it engages, flinging me into a rock outcropping.

d) all of the above.

6. If I were to lure someone to step out from high atop a cliff face, he would

a) comically defy gravity for a few seconds before plunging and hitting the ground with a gentle "poof."

b) survive the fall intact, but subsequently be crushed by the ledge he'd sawed off just before falling.

c) hey, that sounds like fun, I'm gonna go try it!

Scoring: We haven't included any method for scoring. If this makes you so upset that your eyes bulge out and steam shoots from your ears, you watched too much cartoon violence as a child.

Paul

When I was a kid I thought the best thing about being an adult would be that you could go to Dairy Queen and order any kind of ice cream you want. You wouldn't have to settle for a small sundae or a dipped cone . . . you could get the Royal Treat, every time. Hell, you could get two if you wanted. Who's going to stop you?

The answer is: you. Because the problem, of course, is that once you're an adult you don't *want* that much ice cream. You can see it's basically half-melted goopy chemical paste. Sure, you might still gobble down a Royal Treat. But the joy you feel afterwards is outweighed by the guilt. Such is the way of things.

This is the great irony of getting older. As an adult, you've basically won the kid lottery. You can do all the things a kid can't – stay up late, not brush your teeth, browse the comics for free without the store owner saying, "This isn't a library!"

Even if you're broke, by an eight-year-old's standards, you're rich. Say you've only got fifty dollars to your name. That's *fifty dollars!* With fifty dollars you can pretty much go out and buy *any kind of water gun you want.* You can buy *a dozen* Royal Treats.

But of course you never go out and actually *do* any of the

things which, as a little kid, you wanted to do. You go to bed early, you brush your teeth, you pay the gas bill instead of buying many water guns. If anything, you buy fewer water guns than a kid would.

This must seem inexplicable to children. To them, adults are like those lottery winners who win a million dollars but, annoyingly, want to keep their jobs anyway.

The compensation for all this age-related loss of irresponsibility is supposed to be the wisdom that comes with age. But this never seemed true to me. To me, the answers to all the big existential questions seem as far away now as they did ten years ago. When it comes to the BIG QUESTIONS, I basically don't know a thing.

At least, it *seemed* like I didn't know a thing until I got my own kids. Once I started hanging around with a two-year-old, I realized I'm a fountain of useful information and solutions to deep problems I'd forgotten ever having.

Let me give you an example: Say you want what's inside a box. Well, you have to open the box first. This is news to a two-year-old. Here's another one. Why is the pop can spilling? Well, *because you're holding it upside down*. To a two-year-old, this seems insightful. More advice: If you want to open a door, you need to *turn the doorknob*. (Of course you'll want to keep that last bit of knowledge from your two-year-old as long as possible.)

To a little kid, these are the answers to the BIG QUESTIONS. To my two-year-old, I'm the unbelievably wise, box-opening man, a brainiac in the ways of the pop can. I am the doorknob Jedi, mastering the mysterious and powerful door-related forces to open the magic portal – for a few more weeks anyway, until my daughter starts paying a little more attention.

So maybe I don't know anything. But my daughter thinks I know things. Yes, once she's a teen she'll change her mind and think she knows everything and I know nothing. But that's okay, because eventually she'll be in her thirties and she'll realize she doesn't know anything, but by then I'll be a senior, and I'll once again think I know everything, just like I did when I was a teen. Who's laughing *then*?

Also, by that point in the future, they'll probably have some pretty cool water guns, and maybe someone will give me one when I retire.

Things You Know That Will Blow a Two-Year-Old's Mind:

- Right shoes and left shoes aren't interchangeable. Putting the wrong shoe on the wrong foot may lead to discomfort.
- Using a combination of flexibility, mental discipline, and fortitude, you can put on a shirt *by yourself*.
- It's possible to get the last juice out of a freezie using a combination of suction and manual manipulation.
- Like the Death Star, a juice box has only one vulnerability. Only at this single weak point is it possible to stab the straw through the box to gain access to the juice.
- To retain the largest number of peas, spoons have to be held in such a manner that the peas are *on top of* the spoon.
- For some reason, small things won't pass through larger things. Surprisingly, this holds true even if you try repeatedly, each time in exactly the same way.

- The Lego man will not snap into the Playmobil car because, sadly, the systems are not compatible.
- In the alphabet song, the phrase "elemenopee" is in fact the letters "L, M, N, O, and P."
- Grandma's voice will only come out of the phone at certain times.
- Rubbing processed cheese into your hair doesn't make you less hungry.
- It's a bad idea to try to stand up suddenly while crawling under a coffee table.
- A pickle jar will not fit inside your mouth.
- Your Elmo doll is where you set it down forty seconds ago, just inches out of your direct line of sight.

Scott

Midnight used to be mine. The hour of drinks, of too-loud clubs, of hockey games beamed from the West Coast and of Letterman's first guest. The evening was never exactly young at midnight, but it still had its own teeth. It was vital and usually optimistic. We were pals, me and midnight. We saw a lot of each other.

Still do, as a matter of fact. But our encounters now begin with me climbing from bed with a groggy inelegance and awful hair, stubbing my toe, thwacking my face against the door frame, tripping over a wayward Elmo. The abrupt call has come from the bedroom shared by my two young sons: Mommy! Daddy! (or from 18-month-old William, a less specific *bwaaahhh!*). They used to wake up wanting to be fed. I was prepared for that. I heard rumours that babies required sustenance. Now they wake up wanting – what exactly? To wake me up, I conclude in a conspiratorial pique. To laugh at Daddy's muttered profanity and throbbing toe.

Or perhaps it is midnight. Midnight has discovered me in bed and is rousing me to see if I want to come out and play, just like old times.

Alas, midnight doesn't get it. Our relationship is over. Midnight now belongs to my children, to James and William.

Daddy! *Daddy!* I'm hungry. I'm cold. There are nightmares, bedwetting, nightmares about bedwetting – and that's just me! It's exhausting. And yet, at the same time, it is hard not to respect the diabolical brilliance. My children stake a cruel, determined ownership of midnight, they interrupt my sleep, they wear me down. And then soon enough they will become teenagers. Where once I yearned only for a night's silence from their room, I will ache for the sound of their safe return.

Be home by midnight, I'll say, and I'll say, I mean it. I'll be waiting, I'll insist. And my children will smile. Having deprived me of sleep for those many years, they'll know I haven't so much as a hope of staying up that late.

TEACHING YOUR CHILD TO
THINK CREATIVELY

Kids are great at thinking creatively, and, as a parent, you'll want to foster and nourish this creativity, so your child grows into an adult who can go into the world able to think "outside the box."

Experts agree that thinking creatively will be an important asset in the cutthroat job market of tomorrow. In fact, scientists now believe there will be no ideas left inside the box by the year 2010, so it's important your child start learning how to think outside that box today.

In fact, it's so important that your children be able to think creatively that you can't just sit back and let them think creatively – you have to make them think creatively. So creatively that their creative, fun, fanciful thinking will leave other little kids in the dust.

That's why you need to set aside forty-five minutes a week for "creative time." Here's how to do it.

Step One:
Before you can begin to teach your child to think creatively, you'll need a pad of lined letter-sized paper, a well-sharpened #2 HB pencil, a black magic marker, and some three-quarter-inch

transparent tape. You'll also need a highlighter – yellow is best, but blue is acceptable. No pink.

Store all your creative thinking tools in a standard-size document storage box so they'll be easily accessible when it's time to think creatively. (You may wish to hide this box from your children, or to obtain a locking box, to prevent unsupervised creative activity.)

Optional: Using the magic marker, write the words "Magic Time Creative Thinking Treasure Chest" on the top of the document storage box in cursive handwriting. Have your child decorate your creative thinking treasure chest with up to four (4) stars or happy-face stickers. Be sure your child applies the stickers in the proper manner! (One in each corner, approximately half an inch from the edge of the container.)

Caution: Do not allow your child to apply a mixture of both star and happy-face stickers to the same Magic Time Creative Thinking Treasure Chest.

Step Two:

When your child isn't involved in an important school- or church-related activity, inform him that it's almost "Magical Creative Fun Time." Place an egg timer on a safe, level surface and, following manufacturer's instructions, set it to fifteen minutes. Inform your child that Magical Creative Fun Time has begun, and urge him to apply himself.

Note: Before setting the egg timer, ensure that neither your spouse nor another member of your household is in the process of boiling eggs. If eggs are in fact being prepared, return the egg timer to the kitchen and inform your child that Magical Creative Fun Time will be postponed.

Step Three:

Let the fun begin! Retrieve the magic marker, tape, and pad of paper from your document box. Position the paper in a portrait orientation upon a suitable surface (*not* the same surface occupied by the egg timer). Remove a pencil from your storage box. In block letters, write out your child's name on the first line of the pad. Underline it twice. You may use a ruler.

If you or your child is thirsty, have a drink of water at this time.

Step Four:

Now it's time for your child to "show his stuff"! Hand him the pencil and, starting on the third line of the sheet, allow him to sketch a picture of the egg timer. The sketch may seem inaccurate or even "zany." If this happens, do not scold your child. Merely inform him that the sketch is wrong and tell him to try again, beginning on a line farther down the page.

Continue this creative activity for ten minutes. Your child may fidget or become "antsy." If so, inform your child that failing to think creatively is not an option.

Motivate him by telling him creative thinking will allow him to grow up to be a great creative genius such as Mozart or Milton Friedman, inventor of the expectations-augmented Phillips Curve. (Obviously, if your child is a Keynesian you'll substitute an economist such as Roy Forbes Harrod or Sir John Richard Hicks.)

In any event, if bad behaviour continues, give your child whatever medication your pediatrician has prescribed for these situations.

Step Five:
Now it's time to review your child's wonderfully creative endeavours. Using the pencil, your child should place a mark next to his whimsical or "zany" drawings. What kind of mark should he use? A check mark, an "x," even a star – the sky's the limit!

In any case, these drawings are now eliminated.

Step Six:
From your box, retrieve the yellow (possibly blue) highlighter, and highlight the four (4) best realistic drawings of the egg timer. Replace the highlighter's cap and return it to your storage box, along with the rest of your materials.

Before sealing the box, audit the materials to make sure they're all present. You never know when you'll want to think creatively again! (Actually, you do know. Exactly three times a week, until your child is eighteen.)

That's it! You've reached the end of your creative journey for the day! Keep this up and your child will grow into a creative adult, able to think outside the box whenever his employer gives him permission.

At this time you may wish to notify other family members that the egg timer is once again available.

GOING WIGGLY

Scott

"Sold out!" the Web site declared, as it had a dozen times before, and a dozen more before that. I clicked again. The concert was only hours away, and I was determined. Click. Click. Cuss word. Click. Then, magically, as if singled out for heavenly favour by the patron saint of people who should have bought their concert tickets months earlier but were just too damn lazy, a flash of graphics and – success! Print, fold, run. We were off to the show.

I've been going to concerts for twenty years now, and I've never sat closer to the stage than the seventh row. But as we entered the hall, the usher gestured vaguely toward the front. Promising. We walked, getting closer to the stage. I looked at our tickets. I double-checked. And only then was I ready to accept it: After all these years, I'm sitting front-row centre! Euphoria. Then one sudden, horrifying thought: Oh my God, I'm sitting front-row centre – *for the Wiggles!*

As the father of two young boys, I have dutifully read the parenting manuals and marvelled at the reams of contradictory advice. I realize that when it comes to child-rearing, there is no definitive right and wrong, only varying degrees of parental fatigue. And yet, I believe I have discovered the only truly universal maxim of parenthood: A child's affection for a song is directly proportional to how severely it annoys his mother and father.

If, for instance, the song is a gentle folk tune with amusing wordplay and an inspiring message, the child will invariably respond with a facial expression he last made after swallowing mud. If, however, it is a two-minute cacophony of ear-bleeding unpleasantness, a tune that could have been written only by the makers of Advil, devoid of melody and rich in aural toxicity – well then, the child will smile brightly, shimmy about in a reasonable facsimile of dancing and loudly proclaim, "Again!" This is why those discs entitled *Baby's First CD* could just as accurately be called *Daddy's Last CD*: After my mental breakdown, I'll surely be prohibited from handling anything with a sharp edge.

It wasn't always this way. I used to think Elmo was an adorable little rascal. Then I spent six hours in a car with a three-year-old boy who resists sleep the way Ali resisted the draft, and who shriekily demanded relentless playings of his new *Sesame Street* CD – "The green one! The green one!" I listened to Elmo sing with Big Bird. I listened to Elmo sing with Snuffleupagus. And I emerged from the vehicle resolute in the belief that Elmo and all others of his cuddly Muppet ilk should be set loose on the Plains of Nebraska and hunted for sport.

The Wiggles – a quartet of super-square gents from Australia – are, at first glance (and from my front-row perch at the concert, it was a very detailed glance), not especially prone to inducing fatherly thoughts of mass homicide, even though they dress in a manner to suggest they are the only known human kin of the Teletubbies. Each wears a different colour shirt and has a single telltale characteristic: Jeff is always falling asleep; Anthony likes to eat a lot. As the thousands of children obligingly hollered along to the Wiggles's dorky little songs, I marvelled at the brilliance of (a) fashioning a comic routine based solely on narcolepsy and gluttony, and (b) charging thirty bucks a ticket for a stage show that consisted in its entirety of a lame pirate costume and two large boxes.

Had it ended there – had my son ambled home and professed himself sated with all things Wiggly – I might never have needed to reach into that drawer and remove the carving knife. But several weeks had passed, and Wigglemania remained at its insipid zenith in our house. A Wiggles CD in the car, another in the living-room stereo, still another on heavy rotation in the boys' bedroom. The diabolical melodies had infiltrated my subconscious: One day, I dropped the kids off at daycare and drove all the way home without realizing I was still listening to – and, worse yet, humming along to – "Hot Potato, Cold Spaghetti." This had to end.

The CD came in from the car. The knife came out of the drawer. A few well-placed cuts and, next morning, "Oh golly boys, the Wiggles CD is skipping! Tough break!" My victory smile lingered until the voice came from the back seat. "That's OK, Daddy. I'd rather listen to Elmo today anyway."

A Guest Chapter by Dr. Ben Agiter, Child Psychologist
With all the unpleasantness that transpires in this crazy world
– terrorism, poverty, television series starring John Stamos –
these are rather stressful times for those of us with children.
But as taxing and trying as they may be, it is important that we
try to keep open the lines of communication with our youngsters. Remember: It's all about the children. Our beautiful,
fragile children.

For instance, let's say a child were watching television and
heard George W. Bush talking about military action overseas. Well, that would prompt a lot of difficult questions from
a curious young person. Tough questions. Astute questions.
Questions like: "Hey, how did this grade-A doofus get to
be president?"

You may not believe that an adorable little scamp would
ask such a question, but my wife and I have learned from
first-hand experience that even the youngest children are
very perceptive. My own brood is always surprising me with
insightful queries like, "Daddy, if Osama bin Laden despises
the West so much, how come he owns a Handycam?" and
"Daddy, why did you and that stewardess just come out of the
airplane lavatory together?" These are tough questions, and

the truth would only hurt. It may even hurt the children, too.

At this point, perhaps you are skeptical. You might be tempted to inquire: "Dr. Agiter, are you saying we should sugar-coat the world for our kids?" Heavens, no. I am not saying we should sugar-coat the world for our kids. I'm saying we should *lie*. Outright deception is the key to raising a child successfully. If kids ask about Bush, we should say he seized power in a bloody coup. Say he won it in a poker game. Do anything but admit we elected the guy.

And why would we do that? Because my children are ruthless. I mean *all* children. All children are ruthless. They're always looking for signs of vulnerability – for instance, the fact that a man's diploma in child psychology was actually created at home on a dot matrix printer. And when they find that weakness, they exploit it. "Daddy, give me twenty dollars or I'll tell Mom." Or, "Daddy, give me a hundred more dollars or I'll tell Mom."

So in conclusion, let me just say: I get paid $120 for doing this, right?

Scott

Some time ago, *Newsweek* produced a cover story that proclaimed, "TV Is Good for Kids." The magazine also produced a counterpoint, imaginatively entitled, "No, It Isn't." The pro-TV side got significant play, which included flattering images of such iconic merchandise as Elmo and Bob the Builder (they're also TV characters, I'm told), along with a lengthy feature article that included sympathetic, erudite quotations from the obligatory assortment of chin-stroking, pipe-fondling "experts." The anti-TV side got one page. It was written by an austere woman who does not allow her two children to watch television ever, for any reason, at home or away from home, *and that's that missy!* Oh, and did I happen to mention that Mrs. Vader named her girls Jazzy and Gigi? The only thing missing from her essay was a sentence at the end, written in italics, identifying her as "a hippie-dippie whackjob" and relating her dislike for wire hangers.

My favourite segment from the pro-TV piece alerted readers to the existence of a woman who is so impressed by the quality of modern-day children's programming, who is so certain that the furry grouches and animated aardvarks are plumpin' up her kids' brains to an Einsteinian heft, that she installed a TV in the kitchen to enable her young'uns to watch television while they eat. This, I feel the need to remind you, was presented in the context of Something a Responsible Parent Should Do.

MOM: *Don't just watch that* Franklin the Turtle *show. Eat your* Bob the Builder *pasta and drink your* Spider-Man *fruit drink now, Bobby.*

BOBBY (bleary eyed, drooling): *I will, Big Bird.*

I say, why stop there? I say, if there's a TV in the rec room, the bedroom, the kitchen, even the minivan, then why not rig one up in the bathroom, too? I mean, how could you live with yourself as a parent if, some fifteen years on, your portly cathode junkie is rejected at the local community college because you – selfish, selfish you – had failed to nurture his intellectual development by ensuring his bowel movements were conducted in the company of a blue puppet devouring cookies?

Learnin' is, of course, the big thing these days in children's television. CBC, PBS, the specialty channels: They all make the claim that their programming teaches your kids stuff, makes them more enlightened, sinisterly fosters a dominant race of mammothly brained toddlers, etc., etc. And it's true. My kids have learned a lot from watching TV. Specifically, they've learned how to turn on the TV. They've learned that *Blue's Clues* starts around breakfast time. And they've learned that even a few bars of the latest retarded melody from the Wiggles are enough to send Daddy into a blinding, profane rage.

Back when I was a kid, TV didn't need a "rationale" or a "mitigating quality" or a "reason to exist beyond selling lots of crappy toys to our parents." We watched it, we turned it off, we enthusiastically debated why the Wonder Twins only ever transformed into a stupid bird and a useless bucket of water. That was about it. But nowadays, it's all about the alleged educational content. It's okay to let your tykes watch our shows, frazzled parent! You're not neglecting them, you're *helping* them! They're getting smarter and you're getting the opportunity to plan the next corporate takeover or make lunch or mainline heroin. Whatever makes you a better mommy.

I am the father of two young boys. The experience we've had with television is, from what I've learned, a not uncommon one. First kid: We hardly ever permitted him to watch it until age two, and then only infrequently. Second kid: Four of his first ten words were the names of TV characters. In other words, we let things slide a bit – in part because we loosened up as parents, in part because fatigue has sufficiently enfeebled me that I am no longer able to wrest control of the remote from my cunning twenty-kilogram adversary.

When my guys watch TV, I often watch it with them – not out of a stubborn adherence to some parenting scripture, but because I want to enjoy this fleeting phase when we happen to share the same sensibilities: an attraction to cute, furry objects (Elmo, Jim Belushi) and the wisdom to laugh when people fall down and go boom. But here's what I've found: The educational value of a program (and there are some – including *Between the Lions*, *Sesame Street*, and *Blue's Clues* – on which teaching does seem to be a priority) is pretty much irrelevant if you, as an adult, do not sit there and watch the show with your child. Shocking news: Kids are like you! They like to zone out in front of the tube, not necessarily make with the scholarship and enlightenment.

This might sound sarcastic, but it's not meant to. Apart from its ability to sell magazines, does the debate over kids and television really have much in the way of value? Doesn't it seem that the obvious solution, as with many things in life, is moderation. Watching TV can be fun for kids. Maybe they even learn something. Watching too much of it probably isn't a good idea. Does it need to be any more complicated than that?

I fear for the Kitchen TV Kids, soup dribbling down their shirts as they attempt to discern the educational content of the latest episode of *Clifford, The Big Red Dog*. And I fear for Jazzy and Gigi, the two girls for whom television exists only in theory (kind of like Connie Chung's credibility). As they get older, they're going to be mocked for their names and for the pathological manner in which they avoid televisions. Children can be so cruel. Parents, too, especially those who name their kids Jazzy and Gigi and then forbid them from watching any television. The poor girls are going to be so disappointed. One day they're going to rebel. One day they're going to defy their mommy, find themselves a TV, turn it on, and, hearts pounding from the naughtiness of their exploits, finally see what all the fuss is about. Their brains won't melt. Their eyes won't burst and ooze messily. And after a couple hours they'll probably get bored and go to the mall.

It's TV. It's no big deal, unless you want to make it one.

DANGEROUSLY SICK OF WINTER

One side effect of being a new parent is that you rather swiftly come to think of the seasons not in terms of their beauty nor their picturesque representation of the passage of time, but rather in the context of how long it takes to get your child ready to go outside. We are not kidding. The winter months could bring severe cold, relentless snow, power outages, prolonged isolation, famine, societal anarchy, cannibalism, and such other grave misfortunes as the black plague and an all-new Christmas special starring Kathie Lee Gifford – and yet, upon waking each morning, the first thing you would think to yourself is: "Dammit, it's going to take me ten minutes to get Junior into that damn snowsuit."

Spring and fall are times for adorable rain slickers and cute warm sweaters. Summer's status as the desirable, idyllic season is only enhanced by the fact that children need only be affixed with a floppy hat and perhaps a pair of sandals before being permitted to scamper out of doors. You tend to see a lot of naked toddlers in the summertime: running through sprinklers, through wading pools, through Swiss Chalets. This is less a reflection of their own fondness for nudity than it is a sign that, after a long hard winter, parents no longer have the energy to coax a child into a sundress.

Even people who do not have children of their own are familiar with the wintertime routine: A parent struggles to apply a child's sweater, his snow pants, his mitts, his jacket, his boots, his hat, and his scarf only to hear him, within moments of completion of this arduous task, utter the words, "I have to go pee." It should be emphasized that this is simply a natural bodily function – as is the ruptured aneurysm that can subsequently be suffered by the parent. So yes, it's frustrating. But look on the bright side. It could be worse. Instead of saying, "I have to go pee," the child – after being stuffed into sweater, snow pants, mitts, jacket, boots, hat and scarf – could say something like, "Mom, why are you putting all this on me? We live in California." Which would mean parenting had driven you completely crazy, rather than just the partial amount of crazy that comes with applying winter clothes in places where it is actually winter.

The key here is patience. Patience and patience's little helper, Xanax. At all times, the job of dressing a child in winter clothing should be assigned to the parent who is, at that particular moment, the least close to being Dangerously Sick of Winter. Experienced parents recognize there are subtle clues that an adult is becoming Dangerously Sick of Winter, and therefore a useless, quivering mass of shattered nerves, deadened eyes, and extended middle fingers. This affliction can manifest in any number of ways. Perhaps you noticed that your spouse just greeted one of Santa's merry department store elves with a violent kick to the ankle. That could be a sign he or she is Dangerously Sick of Winter. Or maybe your partner rearranged the rooftop Christmas lights to spell, "Up yours." That's definitely a sign, though perhaps not so vivid a sign as the presence of Punxsutawney Phil's head mounted above the fireplace. The parent who is Dangerously Sick of Winter may also derive joy from peculiar sources, such as the realization that while it is not nice to fool Mother Nature, there is no rule to prevent one from punching her in the face. This probably goes without saying, but the parent who is Dangerously Sick of Winter should not engage in any chores that might be considered stressful and therefore likely to exacerbate his condition – chores such as dressing a child to go outside in winter or getting out of bed.

At all times, no matter how frustrated you become, it is important to remember two things: (1) The lyrics to "Stairway to Heaven," and (2) The fact that you are not without options. You could, for instance, move some place warmer. That way, you wouldn't need to attire your child in so many winter clothes. Or you could move some place colder, where you'd have to attire your child in even *more* winter clothes, and then move back to your original house, at which point attiring your child in the original amount of winter clothing would actually feel as though you were attiring them in less winter clothing because you'd been attiring them in so much more winter clothing. Or you could just stay inside until April. It works for bears.

Scott

One of the truly enchanting aspects of parenting – well, "enchanting" may be overselling it, think "interesting" instead, or, if you want to be more accurate, "annoying" – is that even though the shelves of most bookstores are crammed with parenting guides, even though millions upon millions of words have been marshalled to the cause of dispensing invaluable and wise child-rearing wisdom, your child will invariably do something, and quite possibly several things, that no one in the history of human childhood has apparently ever done before. And you'll be on your own. The guides? Worthless. Other parents? Clueless. Your exasperation? Endless.

In our house, this display of singular behaviour had its genesis in the seemingly innocuous matter of – slacks.

Shortly before turning three, James began to take an interest in his wardrobe. Specifically, he began to pay attention to the types of pants we were putting out for him to wear. It wasn't the brand names or the colours that concerned him, it was the type of material. The material from which his pants were manufactured had suddenly become the Single Most Important Thing in the Whole Wide World, surpassing both Lego and his passionately held belief that Kraft Dinner can only be consumed from a bowl, not a plate. It began as a preference. Within days, it had become an obsession. James put it to us plainly: "I only want to wear soft pants."

By "soft pants" he meant sweatpants, the sort of super-soft, ultra-casual trouser typically worn in public by (a) athletes, and (b) people who have pretty much given up on life. For James, no other type of pants would do – and the rattier the better, thank you very much. Khakis were "not soft enough." Corduroys were "too hard." As for jeans – well, jeans had abruptly become the sartorial equivalent of a bed of poisoned, fiery nails. James would certainly not be wearing jeans. "They're hard pants!" he'd holler. "They hurt me." (I began to imagine that were our son to have night-mares, he'd be dreaming that under his bed lurked not a hor-rible, disfigured monster but the chief executive of Levi Strauss & Co.)

It is important to emphasize that his decree on soft pants was not a suggestion, a preference, a simple hankering, or fondness. There would be no negotiation. If we suggested he wear anything other than soft pants, we were rebuffed. If we tried to force him to wear anything other than soft pants, he kicked his legs furiously, he punched, he squirmed, and invariably he wailed. I reasoned and argued and, after endur-ing one especially violent trouser tantrum, bled profusely from the lip. Finally, we relented. We bought several pairs of the nicest hideously ugly soft pants available. He wore them every day. *Every* day. Except in the summer, of course, when he wore . . . soft shorts. For a year's worth of photographs, it looked as though our family consisted of a father, a mother, an adorable baby, and a midget hobo.

Parents who have difficulty toilet training their children tend, in dark moments, to envision a high-school graduation ceremony in which their child strolls proudly across the stage to collect his diploma, a custom-made size-twelve Pamper peeking out above his belt. My wife and I thought of the wedding day: Our eldest son standing alongside his cute young bride, posing for photos attired in an elegant suit jacket, a tailored dress shirt, and grey, ketchup-stained sweatpants.

As a new parent, you are most likely now thinking to yourself, "Well, this will never happen to me" or "I would never let my child do anything so unreasonable." In other words, you're what veteran parents refer to as an Eye-roller. Back before I had children, I was an Eye-roller, too – rolling my eyes whenever I'd see adults catering to the whims of spoiled, grumpy toddlers or failing to prevent their wild, flailing offspring from engaging in public tantrums.

It is only through experience that one comes to realize that negotiating with a young child is like debating a controversial matter of physics with a deaf puma. Kids simply don't understand the ground rules. If you make a good argument, if you introduce an unassailable point of logic, your child will not adopt a beaten countenance and announce: "Touché, good sir. You have bested me again upon this lexical terrain." He will not do this. What he will do is screech "*Arrrrrrrphgnaaa!*" while attempting to gouge out your eyes. For the sake of your sanity (and your eyeballs), you must come to accept this. You must come to accept that, until they reach an age of even modest maturity, children are savage, irrational, and profoundly self-centred creatures. Think of them as celebrities, only smaller.

Confrontation is not the answer. Confrontation is to be avoided. Confrontation will only end in sulking and heartbreak and tears. Definitely in tears. Your child might cry, too.

When the time comes to put on clothes, to put on shoes, to climb into a chair, to do just about anything, my two-year-old pushes my hands away and hollers: "No, me do it!" The problem, of course, is that she can't actually do any of these things. What should I do?

It's normal for a toddler to want to gain some control over her environment. If your child is unable to tie her shoes or put on clothing, it might be best to gently dissuade her from those tasks and let her try other activities. So, for example, next time you're doing your taxes, and your toddler says, "Me do it," let her try. Or you might let her operate a nuclear power plant. That way if things go wrong – and that's okay, it's a learning process – and the auditor or the nuclear power plant emergency guy shows up and they want to know what happened, you can point to your kid and say, "She do it."

My son has developed an interest in playing with guns and miniature soldiers. Should I actively attempt to discourage this?

Miniature soldiers are a good choice for a kid because it's hard for them to get real, big soldiers to do what they say. A gun isn't a great plaything, though. It's better to get, say, a toy gun. Something made of plastic maybe. It's less dangerous. Plastic smallpox virus can also be a fun plaything.

I don't mean for this to sound rude or critical, but my daughter never shuts up. She is always talking, always asking questions. I admire her curiosity, but would it be wrong to teach her that the occasional bit of silence can be golden?

Shut up. I'm sick of your questions.

Our son has developed what we consider to be an unnatural fear of barbers. It's an ordeal every time we go, even if we visit a different shop. What can we do?

He thinks the barber is scary? Take him to the dentist. He'll *beg* you to go to the barber after that. But don't let him. Keep taking him to the dentist, as much as possible. Sure, his hair will be pretty long, but he'll have perfect teeth. He'll be like Fabio!

Our daughter introduced us to her imaginary friend last night. Is it healthy for a three-year-old to carry on a relationship with a non-existent person?

Oh that's cute. Your "daughter" told you she had an imaginary friend. Can we meet this "daughter" or can only you see her? Maybe your "daughter" could hang out with our "friend" the purple elephant? They could go dance with the pixies down by Made-Up Candy Mountain, and drink froo-froo juice, and talk to Pretendo the Made-Up Clown.

For those readers who really *do* have a daughter, and find themselves in this situation, the way to handle it is this: Tell the child that it's nice to meet the imaginary friend, but explain that this isn't a *real* friend – that, in fact, this imaginary person is just coming over to play with her toys and would stab her in the back in a second.

What can I do about my child's incessant nagging and whining?
It seems he's never happy.
You again? We thought we told you to shut up a couple of questions ago. We're tired of your complaining.

Our son is now 26 months old, and even though he is capable of uttering words and short sentences, there are still many times during which we have no idea what he is saying. Is this typical?
It is, and it can be frustrating. It's quite common for parents in your situation to begin to think to themselves, "Darn it all, I just wish my kid could *talk*. I wish she could form complete sentences and clearly enunciate words so that we would never again have to speculate as to what she is trying to say." As a new parent, you should know that feeling this way is completely natural. In fact, it's every bit as completely natural as it is utterly insane.

Let us put it to you this way: Are you sure you want your child to learn how to speak? Are you sure? Are you sure? Are you sure, Mommy? Mommy, are you sure? Mommy? Mommy? Mommy? Mommy? Maaaaaaaaaaaaaaaaah-meeeeeeeeeeeeeee? Maaamaaamaaaamaaaaa-meeeeeeeeee? Mommy, are you listening? Are you listening, Mommy? Are you listening to me, Mommy? Are you listening to me, Mommy? Are you listening, Mommy? Mommy? MOMMY? Are you sure? Are you listening? Are you sure you're listening, Mommy? Mommy! Are! You! Sure! What's that? You are sure? You are? You really are? You really are sure, Mommy? Why? Why are you sure? Why are you sure, Mommy? Why? Mommy, why? Why? Why? Why? Why? Whywhywhywhywhywhywhy? Why? [*Brief pause while child looks at cows out the window of the car.*] Why do cows have heads, Mommy? Why do they? Why? Why? How come they do? How come? How come? Why? Why do they? Are you sure? Are you sure, Mommy? Are you sure you're sure?

I admit it – I developed a bad habit when my child was young: I failed to stop using profanity. Today, I swore at a driver who cut me off on the highway and my son immediately started repeating the word, over and over, at high volume. What's the best way to coax him into not using that expression any more?

First of all, it's important to realize your son isn't swearing at *you*. He's swearing at the driver who cut you off, or possibly at *his* son, if he was riding in the car of the driver who cut you off.

In fact, your son was supporting you, and instead of harping on the negative, you should be a little more appreciative.

Nevertheless, swearing isn't an activity you want to encourage, and so if you want to modify your son's behaviour you will first have to modify your own behaviour. Next time someone cuts you off in traffic, loudly and clearly recite the seven times table. Your son will mimic you, and the next thing you know he'll be a math whiz like that guy in *A Beautiful Mind*.

We hear that is a good movie.

My brother's kids still have two naps a day. My boy, on the other hand, no longer sleeps at all during the day and come nightfall is still full of energy. I admire his verve, but is there an effective method of making sure he's tired when it's time to go to bed?

Your brother's kids have two naps a day because, truthfully, your brother is boring. He talks and talks and talks, shows that slide show from the time he went to Knott's Berry Farm – the guy puts people to sleep. No wonder the kids want to go down for the first nap and, let's be honest, the second nap is probably just a ruse to get away from your boring, boring brother.

You, on the other hand, are an exciting, dynamic person who is fun to be with. You're always doing crazy, fun, exciting things like writing to people with questions about your kids, going over to your brother's to count how many naps his kids take, sitting around admiring your children's verve, etc.

No wonder your kids don't sleep! They don't want to miss an action-packed minute of the party that is your life. And who can blame them? It's hard to believe that you and your brother are even related, because in terms of action, you couldn't be more different.

We wonder if the guy from *A Beautiful Mind* had a brother, and if so, was he good at math too? We really should see that movie.

Our child loves the bath, but goes ballistic if ever we try to wash her hair. What should we do?
You don't want to ruin an otherwise enjoyable bath time by introducing the stress of unwanted hair washing, so the solution is to let your child enjoy her bath, then wash her hair later when she's not in the bath.

When's a good time to wash her hair? When she's doing something she already hates, or if she's having a temper tantrum for some reason. At this point, she's upset already, so there's no harm in suddenly washing her hair vigorously.

This can be tricky to do if she's in the car or sitting in her high chair, but it is possible. Just keep a bucket of warm soapy water around at all times, then the minute she gets upset about something, hold her upside down and dip her head in the bucket. Be sure to swirl her around in a stirring motion so her hair gets nice and clean. Then pull her out, rinse her off with a hose and, depending on the directions on your shampoo bottle, repeat.

Another option would be to take her through the car wash with the car window open, but this could damage your upholstery. You don't have to be a genius like the guy in *A Beautiful Mind* to know that!

We don't want to stifle any potential artistic urges that our daughter has but at the same time we're not keen on having to repaint our hallway on a weekly basis. Is there a way of gently but firmly establishing that crayons are meant for drawing on paper, not walls?
Repaint your hallway? You know crayon washes off, right?

My daughter recently caught a glimpse of a friend's naked baby. The boy was naked and my daughter saw his penis. Now she keeps asking why she can't have one. What should we tell her?
When dealing with issues of sexuality, honesty is often the best policy. That's what the experts say, anyway. We prefer to think that "honesty" is the best policy. "Honesty" is just like honesty, only with more lies. The best part of embracing

"honesty" as the best policy is that you don't have to talk to your daughter about penises – ever! When she asks why she can't have a penis, pretend you can't hear her or tell her you don't speak English, señorita. Let us assure you: telling the "truth" never felt so good!

My son has taken a fancy to picking his nose. The more I tell him it's gross, the more he does it. How do I get him to stop?
This is a great example of the effects of reverse psychology. Tell a child that something is unacceptable and he'll keep doing it. Tell him that something is acceptable and he'll show little interest in repeating the behaviour. As you can probably discern for yourself, there really is only one solution: Whatever you do, don't have children. They'll drive you crazy.

Piece of cake, really. Keep feeding her. Drive him to piano practice. Help her learn to drive. Maybe buy him a new pair of pants every now and then. That's pretty much it. Enjoy!

CONCLUSION: WHAT DOES IT MEAN TO BE A PARENT?

What does it mean to be a parent? Why have children? How many children do you have? Is that your kid there, sticking the dinky car up his nose? From the dawn of time man has asked these questions. Except "dinky car" used to be "stick."

The answers are as varied as human experience. Why have kids? Perhaps you seek the joy and fulfillment that comes with parenthood. Or maybe you feel the urge to carry on your family line, to forge a link in the great genetic chain that stretches from past to future. Perhaps you look forward to the personal growth that goes along with raising a child.

Or maybe you're lonely and your building doesn't allow cats. Maybe you look forward to the laundry challenges that come from having someone regularly throw up on your shoulder. Maybe you simply seek someone who will draw on your new laptop with a felt marker. Or maybe those discount condoms you bought weren't such a good deal after all.

Either way, you're a parent now. An apt metaphor would be that life is a "journey" and children are your fellow "travellers." A less-apt metaphor would be that life is a "salad" and children are your "croutons." A really poor metaphor would be that life is a "battleship" and your children are "chickens."

However you look at it, the challenge of raising kids is certainly outweighed by the reward. Whether you turn your kids over to the authorities in exchange for that reward is up to you.

So try to remember as you go through these first years of your child's life: yes, these are harried and stressful times. Your child will waddle around the house, knocking over things and pulling expensive things off other expensive breakable things which then tip and shatter, causing bits of expensive thing to lodge themselves inside other soft and breakable things.

At this point you may ask yourself: Is it all worth it? The answer is almost certainly no. You paid *way* too much for those expensive things. Especially considering that they got smashed before you got much use out of them.

But in spite of the difficulties, as you look in your child's eyes, you'll see something. Something you've never seen before. And that is the reflection of your other child, sneaking around behind you, about to wreck some other breakable expensive thing, the only one that isn't broken yet. And at that moment, you'll find yourself smiling. Because there's no *way* you can get to the other side of the living room in time to catch that thing and, besides, it belongs to your spouse.

Yes, these are the golden moments. Years from now you will look back on this time fondly – the days when your children were new and small and could do relatively little damage. You will treasure these memories. You'll have to, because anything else you value will have long since been pulled off a coffee table and smashed.

There are many trials that go along with being a parent: the sleepless nights, the frayed nerves, the courtroom trials that come after you turn your kids in to the cops for that reward. But don't forget the benefits. These are:

1. Access to better "mother with child" parking spaces at some malls.

2. Love and fulfillment, blah blah blah.

3. You can go see that new *Rugrats* movie with less embarrassment.

The list goes on and on. Well, actually, the list stops at three, but there's probably a longer list somewhere that goes on and on. Give us a break. Who wants to spend a bunch of time reading some stupid list anyway?

Some aspects of being a parent will always remain mysterious. Why do we have this deep urge to create new life, to bring children into the world and mould them in our image? When is it time to hold children close and when is it time to let them go? And why *is* that kid sticking a dinky car up his nose?

But there's one question that does have an answer. What does it mean to be a parent? Ultimately, it means you're a person who has kids.

And, hey, that's you now! Welcome to the club!

APPENDIX ONE

Sooner or later, unless you learn your lesson, you're bound to repeat your mistake and conceive a second child. If this happens to you, stop and think for a moment about the difficulties you will face raising two children at once.

If you haven't yet packed your bag and headed to the bus station, never to return, read on for some pointers on how to deal with the unfortunate consequences of your ill-advised copulation.

First Step: Do You Really Have a Second Child?

Do you really have a second child? It's not always easy to tell. Someone else's child may have come over to visit yours (they often travel in pairs, and they even form packs for birthday parties). Or, perhaps your child grew and this new child is merely an older version of the child you had earlier.

There are signs you can peruse to tell if you really have two children. One is, Have you been to a hospital recently? If you remember being in a hospital, but your body shows no evidence of recent injury, you or your spouse may have had a baby.

Another good sign is "congratulations on the new baby"-type greeting cards on your mantel. These can be a clue, but it's important not to get carried away – they may be cards that were given to you on the birth of your *first* child which you haven't thrown away yet. (If there are more than three cards, this is probably the case, because by the time a second kid comes along, nobody bothers to send cards.)

Think back over the preceding year. Did you for some reason have sex with your spouse at any point? Or, if you're a man, do you remember someone else having sex with your spouse? Think back: If this happened, you two may have had a conversation about it.

Regardless, the indicators are murky at best. If you see something hanging around your house that appears to be a second child, it's best to assume you do in fact have two children now, and act accordingly. Worst comes to worst, the neighbours come over and wonder why you're painting a spare bedroom for their kid.

Jealousy

It's normal for a first child to become jealous of the new arrival. This jealousy may take a few days to manifest itself, after the novelty and excitement of the new baby has died down.

If your first-born is a toddler, you may see her regress to early behaviours to try to gain your attention. She may cry, or show renewed interest in the bottle or breast. She may even try to lie in the crib. These are all normal symptoms. If, however, your toddler also has reduced in size, has a soft spot on the top of her head, and a fresh-looking umbilical stump, then probably you've gotten confused and *you're looking at the newborn*. Try to locate your toddler.

What should you do about sibling jealousy? Some experts advise that it's best to do nothing; that it will all sort itself out and, ideally, the jealousy will be reciprocated by the new baby, leading to a good bargaining position for you as a parent where you can play them off against one another in an endless competition for your love.

However, a few experts see this as cruel. Presumably the experts in this second group are just poor losers who lost the love competition to their more popular siblings.

If you do want to take steps to deal with a toddler's sibling jealousy, a good approach is to *outdo the toddler* by being even more jealous of the baby. Complain every time your spouse pays attention to the baby. Every time the baby gets a new toy or sleeper, whine and moan that you never get to have any fun any more. If you are a man, attempt to breast-feed. All the time.

Will this work? It might illustrate to your toddler that jealousy, although normal, should be kept under control. But more importantly, your spouse might cave and you might get a present, like a new Xbox or something.

Time Management

What's the best way to take care of two small children, each clamouring for your attention?

If your first child is too young to go to school unfortunately this means he's also too young to be sent off to some sort of military school, which is too bad. The army doesn't seem to want very young children as soldiers – which is puzzling because any parent can tell you preschoolers are relentless and utterly without pity.

So how to deal with two kids? Listen to the words of Sun-Zi, famed Chinese thinker and author of the *The Art of War* – a treatise which, thousands of years after it was first written, is still read by students of everything from philosophy to commerce.

On the subject of children, Sun-Zi says: "I don't have a bunch of children, and so I have enough free time to write *The Art of War*, a treatise which will be read thousands of years from now by students of everything from philosophy to commerce."

Later, Sun-Zi did have several children and penned another less famous piece of writing called "Half-completed shopping list."

Stress on the Spousal Relationship

Taking care of two kids is a lot of work, and it's normal for the stress to carry over into the relationship between the two parents. This can lead to divorce, which in a way can solve the problem because you can just take one kid each, find new partners who don't have their own kids, and you're back to the ideal two adult per kid ratio.

(If you're lucky enough to belong to a polygamist culture, your problems are solved! Grab a couple more spouses, make sure they're infertile, and you're sailing. We envy you, polygamist – you're livin' on easy street.)

Take time away from the kids and spend it with your spouse. Quality time. Go out to dinner. Have a bath by candlelight together. Go away for a weekend. Take the time. You need it. It's important to get away to a quiet private place so you and your spouse can really finish that argument over who forgot to pick up diapers.

If You Have a Larger Family, with Three or More Kids

What are you, stupid? Yes, in the past, families often had five, six, or even more children. But that's because it was the past. People were stupid. They rode *horses*, for God's sake! Have you seen some of the stupid hats people wore back then? People in the olden days were idiots, that's why they had seven kids. Don't you go doing it!

If you've already got three or more kids, there's nothing you can do about it now. Our best advice is to buy a van, teach them each a musical instrument, and tour across the country, spreading musical happiness and optionally solving crime.

APPENDIX TWO

PARENTING 2015
A ONE-ACT PLAY

TV: It's eleven o'clock. Do you know where your children are?

DAD: Hey, that's a good question. What time did you tell Jenna to be home by?

MOM: Me? I haven't even seen her today. I figured she must have talked to you.

DAD (*gesturing to television*): She might have tried. But I got caught up in that Surly Hot-Dog Vendor marathon on A&E. [*chuckles*] I mean, looking back, who'd have thought he'd be the breakout *Law & Order* character who gets his own spinoff?!

MOM: No big deal. I'll page her.

Two minutes pass.

MOM: She hasn't replied. Call her on her wristphone, just to be safe.

DAD (*looks up number and dials*): No answer.

MOM: She's getting to be such a handful. Maybe we should phone some of her friends?

DAD: Good idea.

MOM: So go ahead and do it.

DAD: I don't know their numbers [*pause*] or their names. There's that kind of chubby girl who sometimes comes over. You know, what's-her-nose . . . Fatty.

MOM: Gloria. No, Glory. No, wait . . . remember that time she stayed with us for two weeks? I think I called her Donna.

TV: It's 11:05. Do you know where your children are now? Huh, do you?

MOM: Teenagers these days! So irresponsible. I'm going on-line to check her GPS coordinates.

DAD: Best investment we ever made, that neck-mounted tracking module.

MOM (*typing expertly at the keyboard*): Even with the ensuing chiropractic bills. [*glances at screen.*] Hmm, that's odd. The signal is coming from inside the house.

DAD: Aw, nuts! She must have pried that piece of crap off with a crowbar. I knew we should have sprung for the titanium clasp instead!

TV: It's 11:06. Do you know where your children are? Because if you don't, you really ought to electronically tag them like the feral beasts they are.

DAD (*flicking off the TV*): Listen, all the bars in town have Web cams now. Scan the places where she hangs out and maybe we'll see her.

MOM: OK, which one should I try first?

DAD: I don't know. Wherever she goes the most.

MOM: How should I know where Gina hangs out?!

DAD: Jenna.

MOM: That's what I said. Jenny.

There is a lull in the conversation. Somewhere, a coyote howls.

DAD: OK, no need to panic. This is precisely why we've been paying those monthly fees to the Pentagon for access to the Defense Department spy-satellite grid. Weather permitting,

I'll be able to scan the downtown core in [*checks watch*] eight minutes and fourteen seconds.

MOM (*rolling her eyes*): You're quite the expert. Must be all that practice you get using Uncle Sam's orbital infrastructure to look down women's blouses.

DAD: You gonna make with the wisecracks at a time like this?

MOM: Sorry. You use the satellites. I'll grab the DNA Teen Tracker and try to follow her trail of hair follicles and genetic detritus. And if she's wearing her DigiNikes, I'll be able to engage the Return Home protocols when I get within five hundred metres. Page me if you spot her.

It's several hours later. Mom and Dad sit slumped at the kitchen table. The power in the house is out, the result of Dad inadvertently setting off a debilitating electromagnetic pulse while attempting to activate the homing beacon that, on the occasion of his daughter's sixteenth birthday, he'd installed in Jenna's skull. As the sun comes up, Jenna walks into the kitchen. She is wearing only an oversized T-shirt and her hair is unkempt.

MOM: Ginny!

DAD (*furious*): And where exactly have you been all night, young lady?

Jenna is taken aback. She rubs her eyes.

JENNA: Um, upstairs. In bed. You know . . . *sleeping*. Like normal people do at night.

Mom and Dad stare at each other. Jenna fetches a bowl of cereal and joins them at the table.

JENNA: Why do you guys look so tired?